The A–Z of FIRST AID

IAN ANDREWS RGN IFNA MRSH

The author is a Registered Nurse whose Health Service career has been spent in Intensive Care. He is also an experienced in-flight nurse and has accompanied ill and injured patients across the world. He has a long association with the Voluntary Sector, and is an active member of the British Red Cross.

AUTHOR'S ACKNOWLEDGEMENTS

The author wishes to record his grateful thanks to his friends for their willing assistance with the photographic sessions; individually they are: Margaret Huxtable, Jenny Baldwin, Olaf and Manuela Brellenthin, Helena Venner, Bob, Rachael and Jennifer Kerr. It goes without saying that without the support and help of my family this book would not have been possible; thank you to Carol, Ian, Rebecca, Duncan and to my mother, Jeanette. Finally the author owes a very great debt to his publisher, Sarah Snape, for her help and guidance during this project.

This book is dedicated to you all – thank you.

PUBLISHER'S ACKNOWLEDGEMENTS

The publishers wish to thank Lt. General Sir Cameron Moffat, KBE FRCS, Chief Medical Adviser to the British Red Cross, for reading the final manuscript.

The A–Z of FIRST AID

WHAT TO DO IN AN EMERGENCY

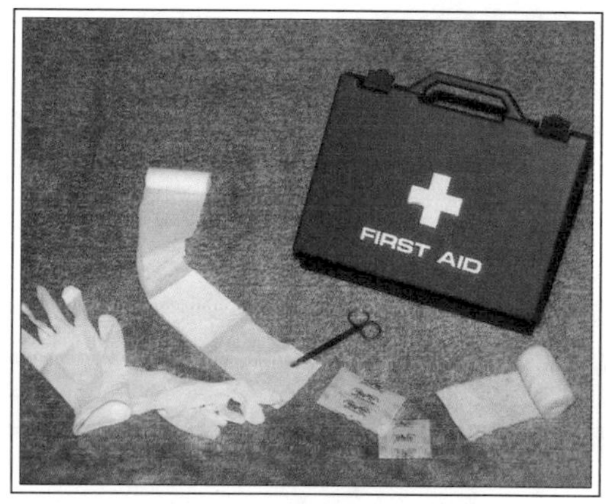

Ian Andrews

BLITZ EDITIONS

Contents

Introduction

About this book

This book has been written as a practical guide to first aid so that **you** can be of use when someone becomes ill or is injured. Familiarising yourself now with the layout of this book will save you time when an emergency strikes.

Main entries are arranged separately and alphabetically from A to Z. These may comprise broad subject headings such as Back Problems, Bone Injuries, Children's Problems, Head Injuries, etc., or individual topics like Baby Resuscitation, Drowning, Overdose, Sprains and Strains, etc. Consult the main Index (p. 142) to locate key topics included within a main subject entry – as, for example, Migraine under Aches and Pains, Cuts in the Mouth under Bleeding, Hiccups under Breathing Problems, etc. In the text, a white cross symbol on a green triangle draws particular attention to crucial procedures.

Keep this book in a handy place, preferably with a first aid kit. Ensure that everyone in the house knows where it is and what to do if the kit is needed.

Introducing first aid

First aid, quite simply, is being able to help someone who is taken ill or who has been injured. Indeed, by following a few simple guidelines, it is possible for **you** to help and perhaps save a life.

Statistically, the most common place for an accident is in and around the home, involving members of your family, particularly children. But no matter where the accident or sudden illness occurs, the same basic guidelines apply.

Safety

Your immediate priority is your own safety, the safety of others and, finally, the safety of the casualty. Too often the automatic response of a person seeing an accident is to run to the scene. This may be courting danger.

Your first actions, then, must be to STOP, LOOK and LISTEN. If you are driving a vehicle be sure to stop in a safe place and use your hazard lights to prevent it becoming a danger to others. Take a little time to look around. What potential hazards can you see? Are others taking appropriate action in response to this emergency or do they pose a risk to safety? While looking, be aware of noises around you. Can you hear anything coming that may involve a further risk?

If you are in any doubt, do not try to act the hero. Ask others to assist or raise the alert by whatever means you can.

Potential sources of danger

- ☐ Vehicles.
- ☐ Spilt fuel, etc.
- ☐ Electricity cables.
- ☐ Gas or other fumes.
- ☐ Falling objects
- ☐ Sharp objects.
- ☐ Chemicals.
- ☐ Water.
- ☐ Fire.

Priorities

Only once you are sure that it is safe to go to the scene should you do so. At all times continue to be aware of the need for safety. If there is more than one casualty, you will have to decide who needs potential life-saving first aid **immediately**. As a rule of thumb, at this stage you can safely ignore anyone who is talking and therefore breathing. You are looking for casualties who are seemingly unconscious or who have life-threatening bleeding. Don't be distracted by someone demanding help. Someone else may need life-saving first aid.

If you are dealing with only one casualty there will be less distraction but you must still identify your priorities. Is life-saving first aid needed or should you concentrate on sending for the emergency services?

Getting help

If others are present, send someone to call for help as soon as possible, with clear guidance as to what type of help you require. If you are alone, sending for help becomes an absolute priority once you have rendered life-saving first aid and your casualty is safe to be left alone.

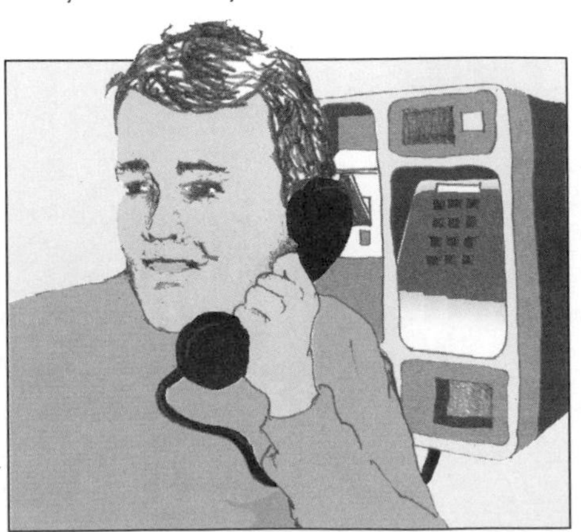

Giving first aid

Once help has been sent for, you can – presuming you have time – continue to give first aid beyond the vital life-giving procedures. Although the arrival of the emergency services may seemingly take for ever, in normal circumstances you will have very little time on your hands before expert help arrives.

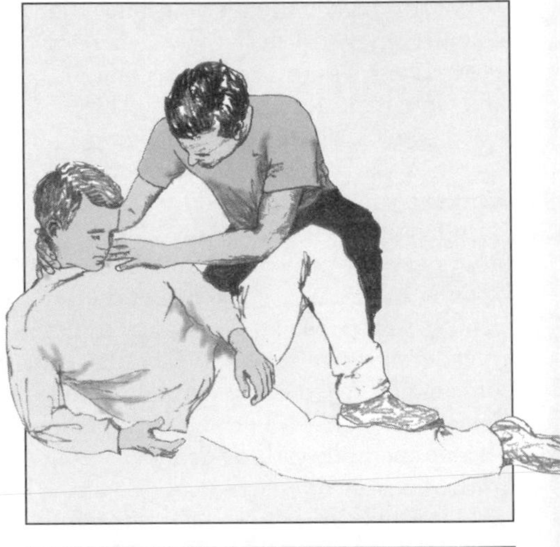

Action in an Emergency

- **Safety** – Stop, look and listen.
- **Get Help** – Dial 999.
- **Prioritise** – Give life-saving first aid.
- **First Aid** – Help where you can.

First aid training

Even though this book is a valuable guide, the very best way of learning about first aid is by taking a course. See p. 140 for details of first aid training organisations and other sources of advice.

Infection Control

Infection control is essentially common sense. While first aid may have to be given without warning and to a complete stranger, it is important to realise that the risk of danger is very, very small. The following advice is the basis of good personal hygiene and also prevents the passage of infection.

Wash your hands as necessary throughout the day.

Keep cuts and grazes covered with a waterproof plaster.

Seek medical advice if you develop any open sores or areas of cracked dry skin on your hands, particularly if you suffer from, or suspect you may have, eczema or psoriasis.

Over recent years many myths have come into being concerning HIV/AIDS. It is not transmitted by social contact. Nor are there any cases of first aiders contracting HIV from giving first aid, including mouth to mouth resuscitation.

When dealing with a casualty

By following the above advice, any chance of HIV transmission is reduced. You can also reduce any possible chance of cross-infection by using the following measures:

If there is time, wash your hands before dealing with the casualty.

Wear gloves (plastic, rubber or latex as found in most first aid kits) when dealing with blood, vomit or excreta.

Ask the casualty, if possible, to stop his/her own bleeding by applying direct pressure and elevating the bleeding part.

Wash your hands after dealing with a casualty.

NO GLOVES ARE AVAILABLE

- Do not withhold first aid under any circumstances.
- Put your hands into plastic bags as improvised gloves, **or**
- Apply direct pressure using pads under the hands.

Cleaning up after a blood/body fluid spill

Wear gloves – kitchen gloves will do if others are not available.

Cover the blood or body fluid with paper towel roll (or similar).

Pour neat disinfectant or undiluted baby sterilising fluid over the towel roll.

Leave for 10-15 minutes.

Use a clean towel roll to mop up the spill – together with used towel rolls.

Clean the area with domestic strength disinfectant.

Dispose of all the used towel roll and the gloves into a plastic bag and seal this.

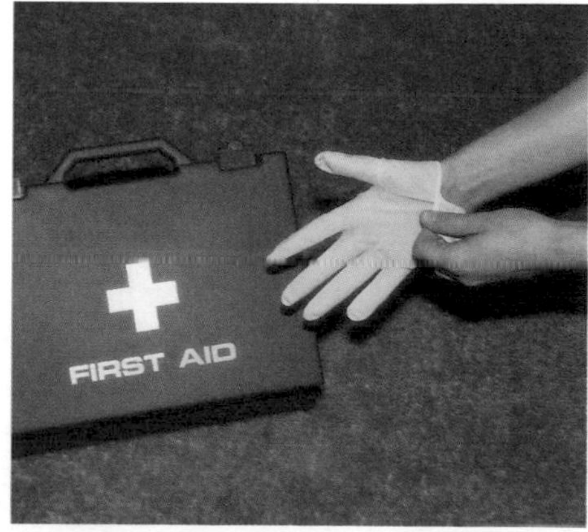

ABC OF RESUSCITATION

(for Adults)

For a person to stay alive there are three essential functions:

The **Airway** must be open so that air (containing oxygen) can enter the body.

Breathing must take place so that oxygen passes through the lungs into the bloodstream.

The heart must **Circulate** the oxygen-carrying blood around the body.
(For the ABC of Resuscitation for Babies and Children, see pp. 15, 19)

Resuscitation for adults

If the casualty appears unconscious or lifeless, the ABC of Resuscitation needs to be performed in order to assess his/her most urgent needs. Once you are sure that there is no danger, carry out an assessment on the basis of the ABC rules. This should be done as quickly as possible following these four steps:

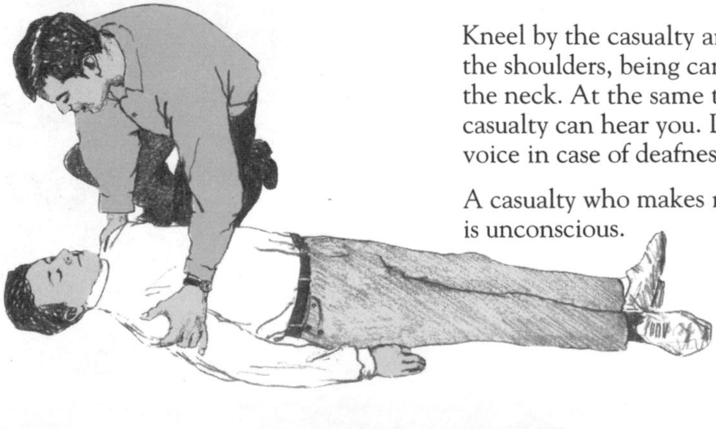

ABC of RESUSCITATION

- Check for consciousness.
- Open the **Airway (A).**
- Check for **Breathing (B).**
- Check for **Circulation (C).**

Check for consciousness

Kneel by the casualty and gently shake the shoulders, being careful not to move the neck. At the same time ask if the casualty can hear you. Do this in a loud voice in case of deafness.

A casualty who makes **no response** at all is unconscious.

A casualty who is semi-conscious will make some sort of response. This may be by opening or flickering the eyes or by making some sort of movement or sound.

Open the airway (A)

Gently look into the casualty's mouth for any obvious blockage, i.e. food or loose dentures (leave well-fitting dentures in place). If you can see something, try to hook your finger **behind** the object so as to pull it out. (If this is not possible, see p. 11.) Avoid poking your finger into the casualty's mouth and potentially pushing the obstruction further down the airway.

Lift the casualty's chin. Do this by placing two fingers under the point of the chin and lifting to bring the chin forward. At the same time place your other hand on the casualty's forehead, tilting the head back. If you suspect a spinal injury be careful to tilt the head gently and only as far as is necessary to open the airway.

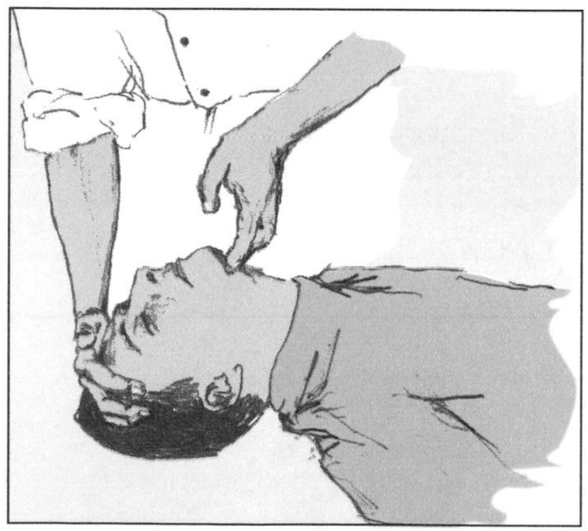

Check for breathing (B)

Keep the casualty's airway open, as described above. Looking at the casualty's chest, place the side of your face close to his/her mouth and nose and try to detect signs of breathing. Do this by simultaneously **looking** for chest movement, **listening** for sounds of breathing and **feeling** for breath on your cheek.

Check for breathing for **5 seconds:** count from 1 to 5. Only at the end of this time should you be able to decide whether or not the casualty is breathing.

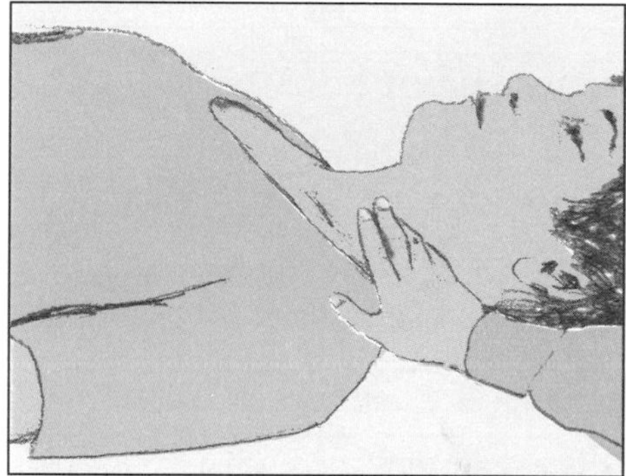

Check for circulation (C)

Using only two fingers of one hand, find the Adam's apple and then slide them sideways into the hollow next to the Adam's apple. Feel here for the carotid pulse (**do not** feel for a pulse at any other place). Remember to press firmly, but without pushing too hard.

Check for the pulse for **5 seconds:** count from 1 to 5 before deciding whether the pulse is present or absent.

Act appropriately

Once you have completed the ABC check, you will be able to decide on your priorities and take the action most appropriate to the casualty's needs. Proceed according to the chart on p. 8.

NO PULSE, NO BREATHING	1. Dial 999 for an ambulance 2. Start resuscitation (p. 6)
NO BREATHING BUT HAS A PULSE	1. Give 10 breaths to the casualty (p. 10) 2. Dial 999 for an ambulance 3. Repeat ABC checks (p. 7) 4. Continue breaths
UNCONSCIOUS *breathing and has a pulse*	1. Treat any life-threatening injury 2. Put the casualty into the recovery position (right) 3. Dial 999 for an ambulance 4. Regularly check the casualty's breathing
CONSCIOUS *breathing and has a pulse*	1. Give first aid as needed 2. Get help as appropriate

Following the chart gives your casualty **the very best chances** of survival. Of course, if someone is assisting you, send for help immediately.

Life-saving first aid

Once you know whether there are any problems following your ABC check, you must give the appropriate life-saving first aid quickly.

The recovery position

This is used for any casualty who is unconscious, breathing and has a pulse – even if you suspect a spinal injury. In the recovery position, the casualty's airway is kept open and any fluids in the mouth drain out rather than into the lungs. The position is very stable and easy to achieve. Before proceeding, remove the casualty's glasses (if worn) as well as any large articles from the pockets.

Kneel beside the casualty and gently tilt back the head. Straighten the legs so that turning is easier.

Place the casualty's arm which is closest to you at a right angle away from the body, with the elbow bent so that the back of the hand lies flat against the ground. ***Do not*** force the hand on to the ground. Find the position where this naturally occurs. For some, the arm may adopt a near 'saluting' position whereas, for others, it may be nearly straight.

Bring the casualty's other arm across his/her body so that the hand rests on the opposite shoulder. **Slide** your hand on to the upper part of that arm and do not let go, otherwise the arm will fall away.

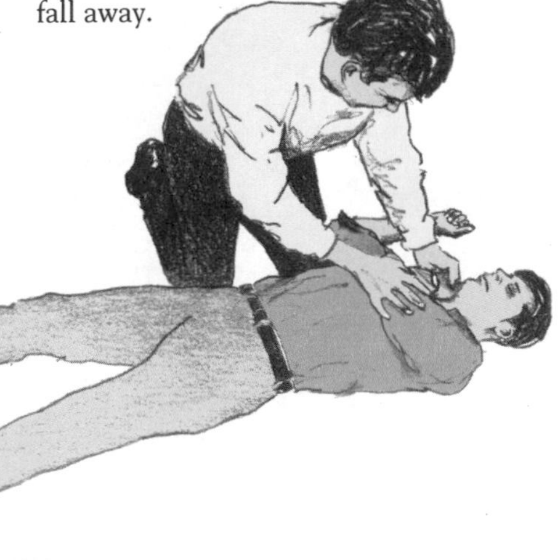

Using your free hand, grasp the casualty's outer thigh (just above the knee) on the leg farthest away from you. Pull the knee up until the foot of that leg rests alongside the casualty's other knee. Ensure that the foot is flat on the ground.

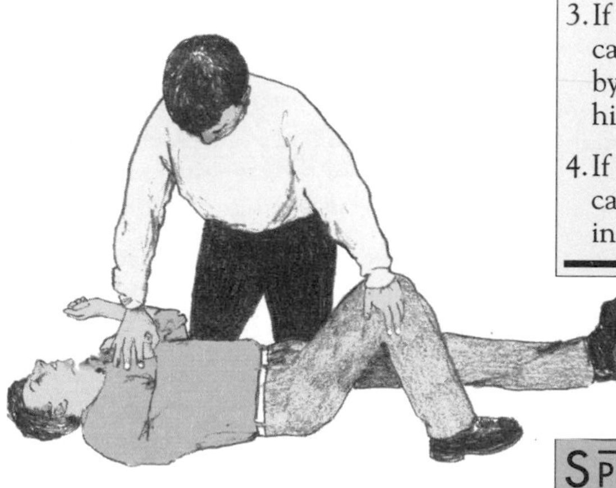

Roll the casualty on to their side by gently pulling at the thigh while supporting the arm.

Once on the side, tilt back the casualty's head so as to ensure a clear airway. If necessary, place one or both of the casualty's hands under his/her head so as to maintain this position. Check to see that the casualty is breathing.

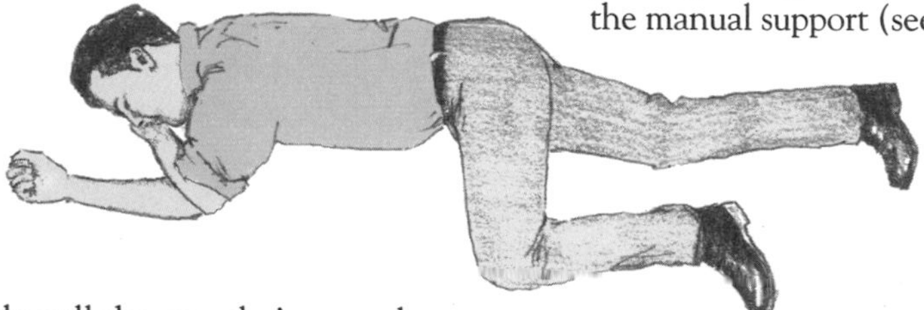

Gently pull the casualty's upper leg so that it is at right angles at the hip and knee.

Check the casualty's breathing and pulse frequently while waiting for an ambulance to arrive.

1. If the casualty is already on his/her side, adjust this position to ensure an open airway and stability.
2. If the casualty has a chest injury, roll him/her **on to** the injured side.
3. If the casualty has injured limbs that cannot be bent, use padding or a bystander's assistance to prevent him/her from rolling face down.
4. If you have to leave an unconscious casualty alone, **always** leave him/her in the recovery position.

SPINAL INJURIES

If you suspect that an unconscious casualty may have a spinal injury then the priority is to ensure that he/she can breathe. If you are by yourself, turn the casualty gently into the recovery position. If you have someone to help, ask this person to support the casualty's head so that the head stays in line with the body during the turn and, once in position, use padding to supplement (but not replace) the manual support (see p. 132).

Breathing for a casualty

When breathing has stopped, it is essential that you start to breathe for the casualty. This is called artificial ventilation. By doing this you deliver air that contains oxygen into the lungs, where it can be taken into the blood and circulated around the brain and body.

Remember: if you are by yourself, give 10 breaths (see below), go and phone for an ambulance and then return to continue resuscitation. Check the ABC of Resuscitation again to ensure that the casualty still has a pulse. If the pulse is now absent you will need to combine chest compressions (p. 12) with artificial respiration.

If the casualty starts to breathe, place in the recovery position and keep a very close eye on his/her condition until help arrives. Check breathing and pulse at very frequent intervals.

You can breathe for someone else by a variety of methods, but the most widely taught is the 'mouth to mouth' method.

Mouth to mouth breathing

Place the casualty flat on his/her back and kneel alongside. Open the airway by lifting the chin and tilting the head.

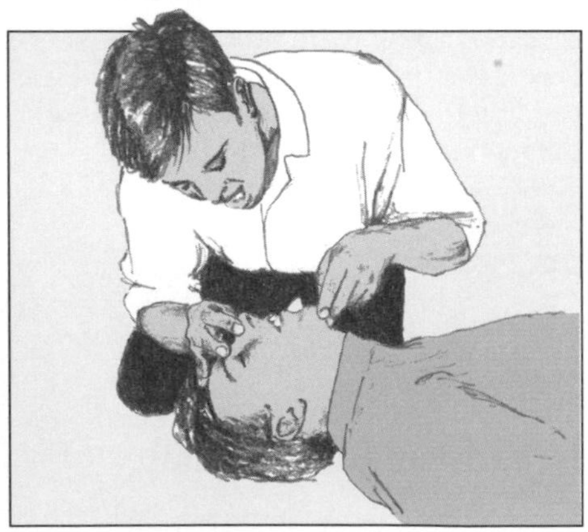

With the hand that is on the casualty's forehead, use the first finger and thumb to pinch the nose closed.

Take a deep breath. Cover the casualty's mouth with yours, ensuring a good seal and then blow slowly but steadily until you see the chest rise; this should take about 2 seconds. ***Do not*** try to inflate the chest any faster than this, or much of the breath will enter the stomach and cause the casualty to vomit.

Remove your mouth from the casualty's and sit back up that you can breathe in 'fresh' air with plenty of oxygen in it. Check also that the casualty's chest falls as the lungs deflate.

Give further breaths in the same manner at a rate of **10 breaths per minute** until the casualty starts to breathe normally, or help arrives.

After every 10 breaths, check to see that the casualty has a pulse in the neck. If not, you will need to start performing chest compressions as well (see p. 12).

HIV/AIDS

- **There has been no incident worldwide of a person becoming HIV positive after breathing for someone else.**

OTHER METHODS OF BREATHING FOR SOMEONE ELSE

- **Mouth to nose** – Instead of breathing into the casualty's mouth, you use the nose. You must open the airway by lifting the chin and tilting the head. The casualty's mouth must be kept closed during mouth to nose breathing.
- **Mouth to mouth and nose** – This is the preferred method for babies and small children (see p. 16).

- **Mouth to stoma** – People who have had their voice boxes removed are left with an opening (stoma) in the neck through which they breathe. Sometimes these people are referred to as 'neck breathers'. There is no need to perform the open airway manoeuvre on neck breathers but it is necessary to seal the mouth and nose while you are blowing into the stoma. Release the mouth during the breathing out phase.

The chest does not rise

It is very important to ensure that the casualty's chest rises as you are blowing in. If the chest does not rise, check:

- The airway is open – chin is lifted, head is tilted.
- You are pinching the casualty's nose shut and have a good seal around the mouth.

Now try a further breath. If the chest does not rise, suspect that there is an obstruction in the casualty's air passage.

Look inside the mouth; if you can see an obstruction try to hook your fingers behind it so as to sweep it out.

Be careful not to push the object farther into the airway or touch the back of the throat.

If this fails, give up to **5 backblows** (if you are able to roll the casualty), proceeding as follows:

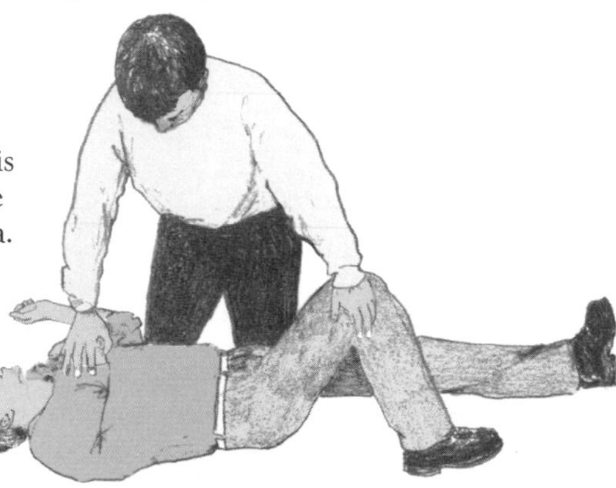

Pull the casualty towards you until you can easily perform the backblows. ***Do not*** let the casualty roll face down. Prevent this by rolling him/her on to your knee(s.)

Identify the area between the casualty's shoulder-blades.

Use the flat of your hand to give up to **5 sharp blows** between the shoulder-blades.

Check to see if any obstruction has come up into the casualty's mouth.

If the backblows fail or you are unable to roll the casualty, you will need to give **abdominal thrusts.** Proceed as follows:

With the casualty flat on his/her back, kneel astride the casualty's upper thighs.

Put the heel of one hand midway between the navel and the ribcage and place your other hand over the first hand.

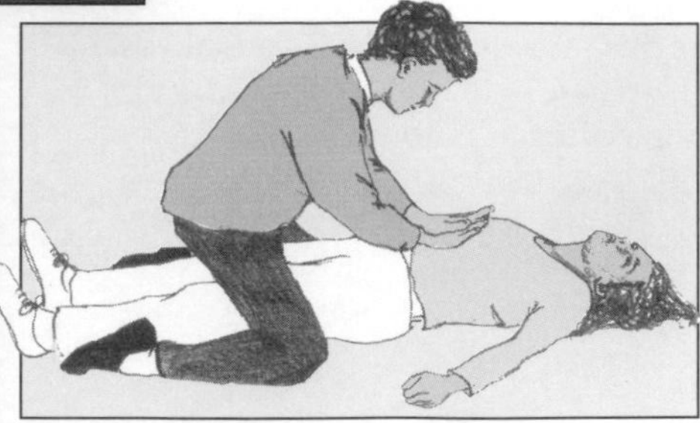

Push sharply inwards and upwards under the casualty's ribcage. Give up to 5 abdominal thrusts.

Check to see if any obstruction has been dislodged into the casualty's mouth.

If an obstruction is visible, try to hook your fingers behind it so as to sweep it out.

If this also fails, try again to breathe for the casualty, this time blowing harder to dislodge the obstruction or at least get air past it.

If this fails, repeat the cycle of 5 backblows, 5 abdominal thrusts and mouth to mouth breathing until the airway clears or help arrives.

> *Do not* use the abdominal thrust (also called the Heimlich Manoeuvre) on very young children or babies (see pp. 17, 21.)

Chest Compressions

When a casualty's pulse has stopped, it means that the heart, too, has stopped. In this situation you need to combine breathing for him/her with chest compressions so that blood can be circulated to the brain, lungs and heart. This is called Cardio-Pulmonary Resuscitation (CPR).

THE SEQUENCE OF CPR

- **REMEMBER!** Dial 999 first.
- Give the casualty 2 breaths.
- Start chest compressions.

Kneel beside the casualty who must be flat on his/her back and on a firm surface. If necessary, drag the casualty on to the floor, trying to protect the head. If it is not possible to lie the casualty flat, you must attempt CPR with the casualty in the position in which he/she was found.

Use the first and second fingers **of one hand** (hand A) to find the casualty's lowest rib. Now slide your fingers along the line of the rib upwards and into the centre of his/her body to where the ribs join the breastbone. Place one finger in this notch and the other, higher, finger on to the breastbone.

Place the heel of your other hand (hand B) on to the breastbone and slide it down until it rests **next** to your finger. **This is where you will push down.**

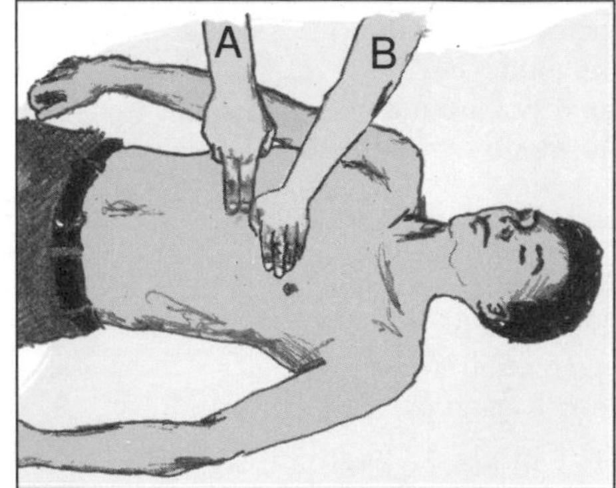

Place hand A on top of hand B and interlock your fingers (see illustration p. 13). Lift your fingers off the casualty's chest so that only the heel of your lower hand B remains in contact with it.

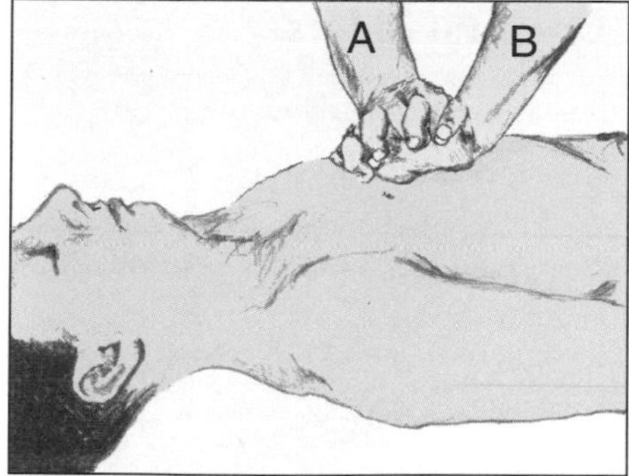

Kneel up to your full height and lean over the casualty with your arms 'locked' straight. Press down vertically so that you depress the breastbone 1-2 in (4-5 cm).

Release the pressure without removing your hands from the casualty's chest. Repeat the compressions at a rate of approximately 80 per minute. Perform CPR in the appropriate sequence as given on p. 14.

If you see any sign of life, perform the ABC check and respond as appropriate.

> To help you give the correct amount of chest compressions it is useful to count as you compress. Try to count '1 and 2 and 3 and 4 and 5' etc., at a moderately brisk rate. Press down on each number, release the pressure on 'and'.

When to stop CPR

- When the casualty's pulse returns.
- When the ambulance service takes over.
- When you are physically exhausted.

If the casualty's pulse returns, check for breathing. If not present, go on breathing for the casualty.

Remember to check for a pulse after every 10 breaths.

Special notes for two-person CPR

- Work on opposite sides of the casualty. The person performing the chest compressions should make a 'count' that the other person can hear. This should be '1 and 2 and 3 and 4 and 5' said at a moderately brisk marching rate.
- Using the count as a guide, give artifical ventilation on the 'and' following the number 5. Pause briefly to allow the chest to rise. Once this has happened, start the next cycle of five chest compressions. ***Do not*** wait for the chest to fall before giving the next chest compression.

Signs of life returning

If you see any sign of life while performing CPR you must not assume that the casualty has recovered. Only infrequently will a casualty make a spontaneous recovery without needing the specialist care delivered by paramedics or doctors.
If you do see any sign of life, i.e. flickering of the eyelids, attempts to breathe, coughing, movement of limbs, etc., **stop the CPR and perform the ABC of Resuscitation.** If the pulse is absent, resume CPR without delay. If the pulse has returned, you may need to continue with artificial ventilation if breathing has not recommenced. Remember to check the carotid (neck) pulse every 10 breaths whilst giving artificial ventilation.
If the casualty starts to breathe unaided, place into the recovery position. Check the casualty's breathing and pulse every 2-3 minutes.

One first aider

Dial 999 for an ambulance as a priority.

Give 2 breaths of artificial ventilation.
Give 15 chest compressions.
} **one cycle of CPR**

Continue CPR cycles until help arrives or the casualty's pulse returns.

Two first aiders

One first aider dials 999 as a priority.

The other gives 2 breaths of artificial ventilation.
Gives 15 chest compressions.
} **one cycle of CPR**

Repeat this cycle until the other first aider returns **THEN:**

One first aider gives one breath.
The other gives 5 chest compressions.
} **one cycle of CPR**

Repeat this cycle until help arrives or the casualty's pulse returns.

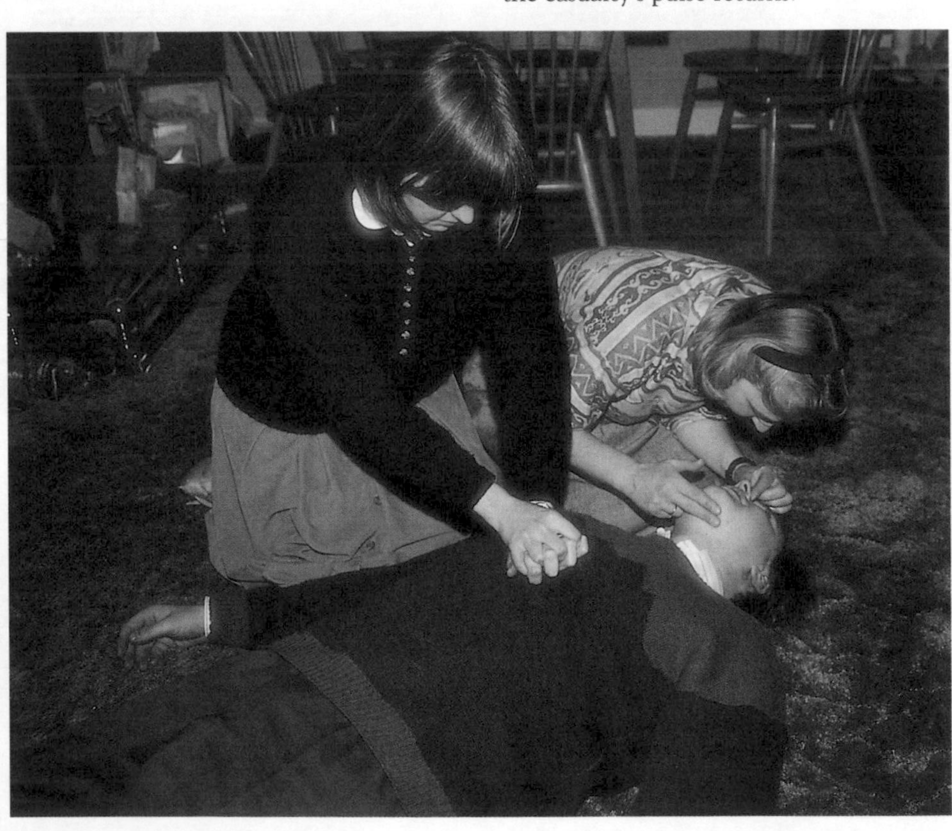

Baby Resuscitation

(Up to 1 year old)

Whereas the techniques for resuscitating a baby are broadly the same as those used for resuscitating a child or adult, there are noticeable differences. Babies (like children) do not suffer heart attacks and sudden cardiac arrest (except in a few rare cases). However, for a variety of reasons babies do stop breathing and, as a result of this, the heart may stop a few minutes later. Because of this, the ABC of Resuscitation has different priorities for a baby.

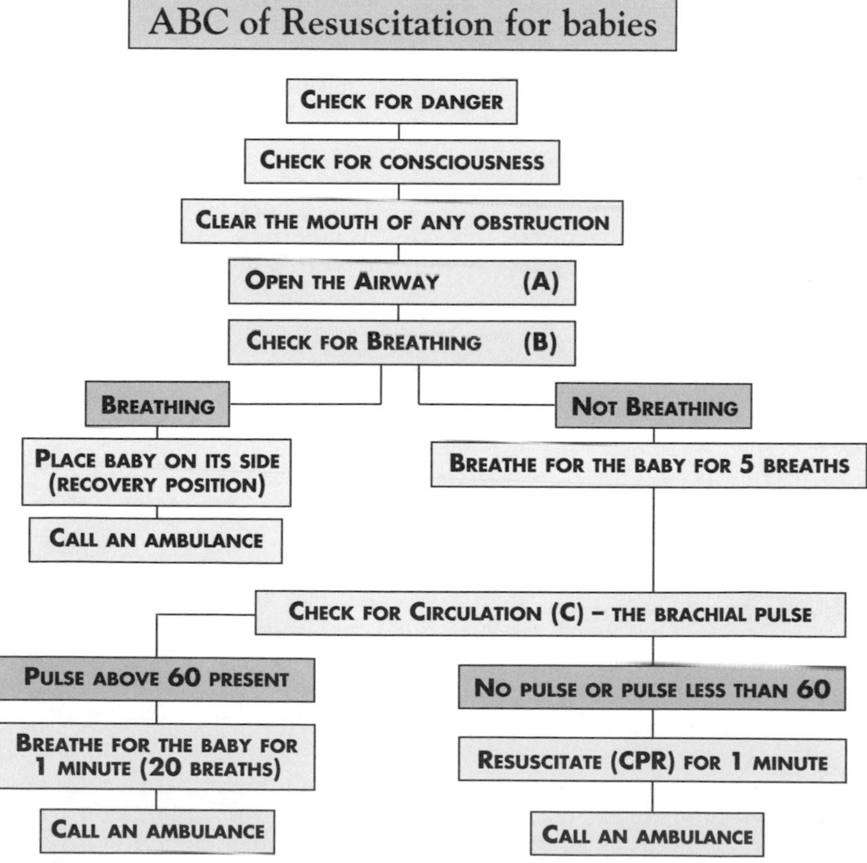

Check for consciousness

Gently shake the baby's shoulders and call out its name.

Open the airway (A)

Check in the baby's mouth for any obvious obstruction. If anything is seen, scoop it out, being very careful **not** to touch the back of the baby's throat.

Lift the baby's chin. Do this by placing one finger under the point of the chin, lifting it to bring the chin forward. At the same time, place the other hand on the baby's forehead. Tilt the baby's head back **very slightly** (do not push the head right back, as this will block the airway).

Check for breathing (B)

Keep the baby's airway open, as described above. Looking at the baby's chest, put the side of your face down close to the mouth and nose and try to detect any signs of breathing. Do this by simultaneously **looking** for chest and tummy movement, **listening** for sounds of breathing and **feeling** for breath on your cheek.

Check for breathing for **5 seconds**: count from 1 to 5. Only at the end of this time should you decide if the baby is breathing or not.

IF THE BABY IS BREATHING

- Put baby into the recovery position (p. 18), or on his/her side with a blanket behind the back.

Breathing for the baby

If the baby is **not breathing** proceed as follows:

Keep the baby's airway open, as already described.

Take a normal breath and seal your mouth over the baby's mouth and nose. Blow in gently until you see the baby's chest rise.

Take your mouth away from around the baby's nose and mouth. Let the baby's chest fall.

Repeat this process four more times with an interval of 3 seconds between each breath (rate of 20 breaths per minute).

The chest does not rise

It is very important that you see the baby's chest rise as you blow in. If the chest does not rise, do the following:

- Lift the chin and tilt the head **very slightly.**
- Check that you have a good seal around the baby's nose and mouth.

Now try a further breath. If the chest does not rise, you must suspect that there is an obstruction in the baby's air passages.

Look inside the mouth. If you can see an obstruction, try to hook your fingers behind it so as to sweep it out. **Be careful not to push the object further into the airway or touch the back of the baby's throat.**

If this fails, give up to **5 backblows**. Do this as follows:

Pick up the baby and place it head-first along your forearm, supporting it against your body and firmly holding its jaw so as to support the head. The baby's head must be lower than its trunk.

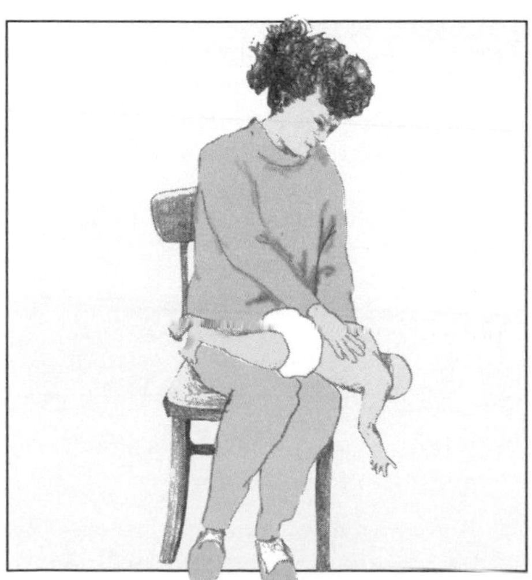

Give up to 5 sharp back blows **between** the baby's shoulder-blades (use the flat of your hand).

Check to see if any obstruction has come up into the baby's mouth.

If the backblows fail you will need to give up to 5 chest thrusts. **Do not perform abdominal thrusts** (p. 12) **on a baby.** Do the following:

Turn the baby on to its back and support it in a head-down position, if possible.

Draw an imaginary line between the baby's nipples. Place two fingers from your free hand on the breastbone approximately one finger's breadth below this imaginary line (this is where you will do the chest thrusts).

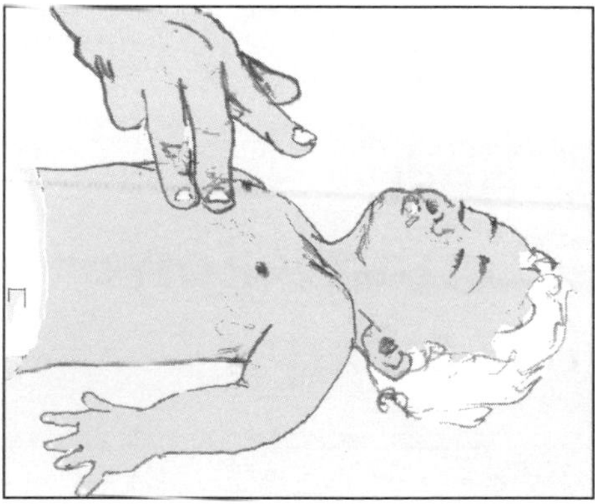

Push down up to 5 times at this position to a depth of $^1/_2$-1 in (1-3 cm).

Check to see if the obstruction has come up into the baby's mouth.

If this fails, try again to breathe for the baby, this time blowing harder to try to dislodge the obstruction or at least get air past it.

If this also fails, repeat the cycle of backblows, 5 chest thrusts and mouth-to-mouth-and-nose breathing (p. 16) until the airway clears or help arrives.

Check for circulation (C)

This is done at the brachial artery in the inside of the baby's upper arm – **not in the baby's neck**.

Using two fingers, find the position on the inside of the baby's upper arm, midway between the shoulder and elbow.

Check for a pulse for 5 seconds before deciding if the pulse is absent.

If you can feel a pulse, count its rate for 30 seconds; double the number so as to give you a pulse rate per minute.

SEQUENCES OF RESUSCITATION

- **No breathing, pulse (over 60 beats per minute) present:** Give 20 breaths per minute.

NB Check for a pulse every minute.

- **No breathing, no pulse (or pulse under 60 beats per minute):** 5 compressions to 1 breath at rate of 100 compressions per minute.

Chest Compressions for a Baby

WHEN TO GIVE CHEST COMPRESSIONS

- When there is no pulse present.
- When the pulse is less than 60 beats per minute.

Ensure the baby is lying on a firm surface.

Place the tips of two fingers on the baby's breastbone one finger's breadth below an imaginary line that runs between the nipples (p. 17).

Press in to a depth of $^1/_2$-1 in (1-3 cm) at a rate of 100 compressions per minute.

Recovery Position for Babies

Unconscious babies need to have their airways protected in the same way as for adults and children.

Place the baby on his/her side with a rolled-up blanket (or similar) behind the back; if necessary, tilt the head back very slightly to ensure an open airway.

Check the baby's breathing at frequent intervals.

WHEN TO TELEPHONE FOR AN AMBULANCE

- If resuscitation is needed – after 1 minute of resuscitation.
- If unconscious – after placing the baby in the recovery position.

Child Resuscitation

(Over 1 year old)

While the techniques for resuscitating a child are broadly the same as those used for resuscitating a baby or adult, there are noticeable differences.

Children (like babies) do not suffer heart attacks and sudden cardiac arrest (except in a few rare cases). However, for a variety of reasons children do stop breathing and as a result of this, the heart may stop a few minutes later. For this reason, the ABC of Resuscitation has different priorities for a child.

The upper age limit for resuscitating a casualty by using child techniques, as opposed to adult techniques, depends on the size of the casualty in comparison to the size (and therefore the strength) of the first aider. A small adult confronted with an unconscious 6-foot lad (who is known to be only 12) should use adult resuscitation techniques.

Check for consciousness

Gently shake the child's shoulders and call out its name.

Open the airway (A)

Check in the child's mouth for any obvious obstruction. If anything is seen, scoop it out using one or two of your fingers; be very careful **not** to touch the back of the child's throat.

Lift the child's chin. Do this by placing two fingers under the point of the chin, lifting it to bring the chin forward.

At the same time, place your other hand on the child's forehead. Tilt the head back **slightly** (do not push the head right back, as this may block the airway).

Check for breathing (B)

Keep the child's airway open, as described above. Looking at the child's chest, put the side of your face down close to the child's mouth and nose and try to detect any signs of breathing. Do this by simultaneously **looking** for chest and tummy movement, **listening** for sounds of breathing and **feeling** for breath on your cheek.

Make this check for **5 seconds:** count from 1 to 5. Only at the end of this time should you decide if the child is not breathing.

IF THE CHILD IS BREATHING

- Put the child into the recovery position (p. 23).

Breathing for the child

Keep the child's airway open, as already described, and pinch the nose closed.

Take a normal breath and seal your mouth over the child's mouth. Blow in gently until you see the child's chest rise.

Take your mouth away from around the child's mouth. Let the child's chest fall.

Repeat this process four more times with an interval of 3 seconds between each breath.

For small children use mouth-to-mouth-and-nose (as for babies, p. 16).

ABC of Resuscitation for children

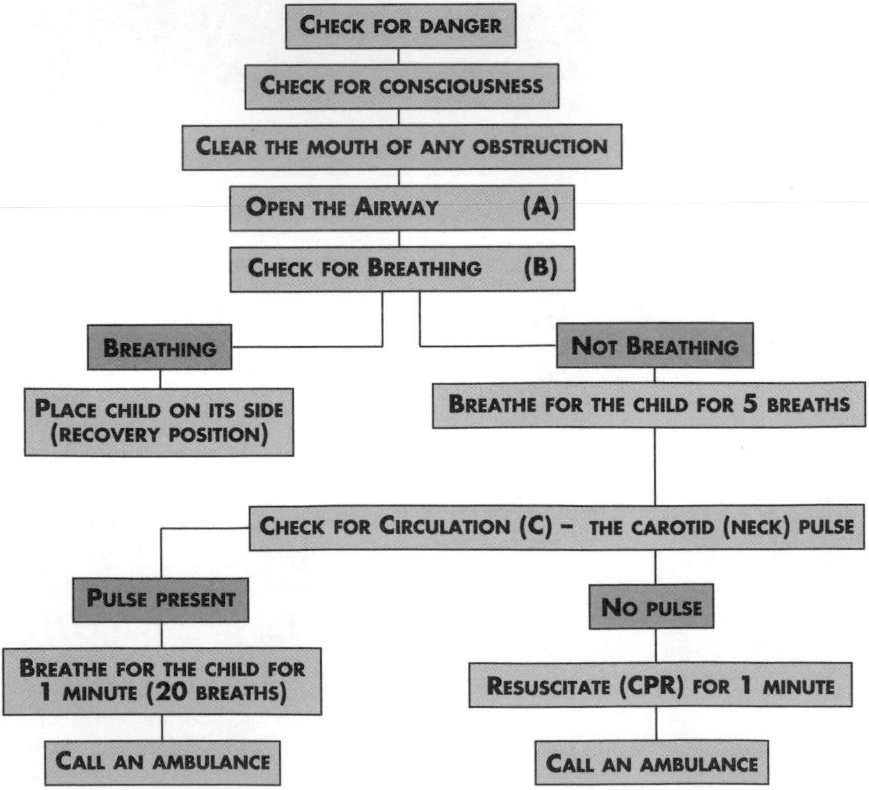

CHECK FOR DANGER

CHECK FOR CONSCIOUSNESS

CLEAR THE MOUTH OF ANY OBSTRUCTION

OPEN THE AIRWAY (A)

CHECK FOR BREATHING (B)

BREATHING

PLACE CHILD ON ITS SIDE (RECOVERY POSITION)

NOT BREATHING

BREATHE FOR THE CHILD FOR 5 BREATHS

CHECK FOR CIRCULATION (C) – THE CAROTID (NECK) PULSE

PULSE PRESENT

BREATHE FOR THE CHILD FOR 1 MINUTE (20 BREATHS)

CALL AN AMBULANCE

NO PULSE

RESUSCITATE (CPR) FOR 1 MINUTE

CALL AN AMBULANCE

The chest does not rise

It is important that you see the child's chest rise as you blow in. If the chest does not rise, do the following:

- Lift chin and tilt the head **slightly.**

- Check that you have a good seal around the child's mouth (and nose).

Try a further breath. If the chest does not rise, you must suspect that there is an obstruction in the child's air passages.

Look inside the mouth. If you can see an obstruction, try to hook your fingers behind it so as to sweep it out. **Be careful not to push the object farther into the airway or touch the back of the child's throat.**

If this fails, give up to **5 backblows**. Do as follows:

Ensure the child is head down, i.e. over your knee.

Give up to 5 sharp backblows **between** the child's shoulder-blades (use the flat of your hand).

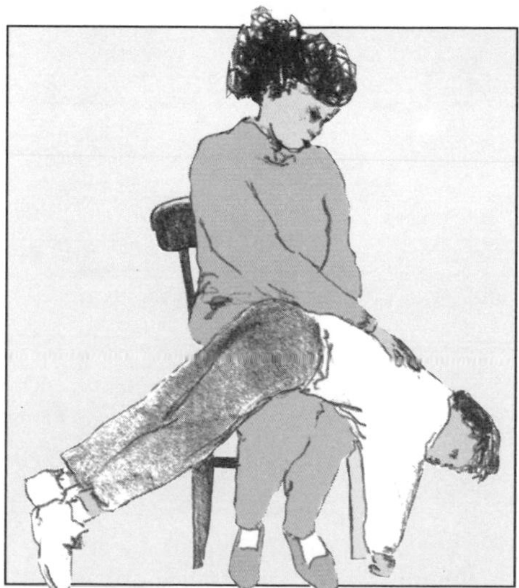

Check to see if any obstruction has come up into the child's mouth.

If the backblows fail you will need to give up to 5 chest thrusts. **Do not perform abdominal thrusts on a very young child.** (For older children it is safe to use the abdominal thrust technique as described on pp. 11-12.) Do the following:

Turn the child on to its back.

Use the first and second fingers of one hand to find the position where the child's lower ribs meet the abdomen. Now slide your fingers up the line of the ribs to the notch where the ribs meet the breastbone. Place one finger in the notch and move the adjacent finger to touch it, positioning it on the breastbone.

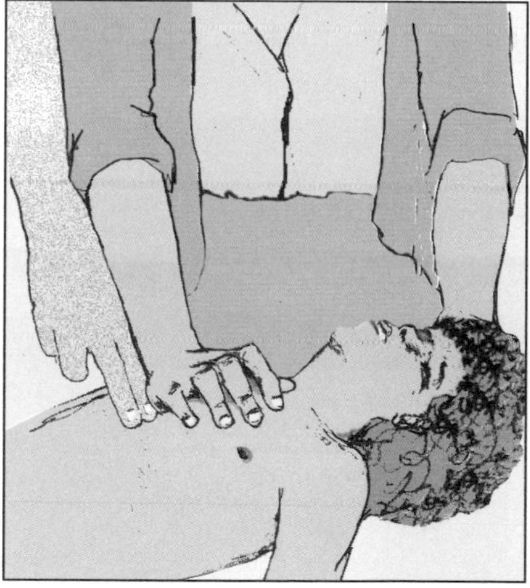

Place the heel of the other hand on to the breastbone immediately next to the fingers; this is the place at which you will press down.

Push down sharply up to 5 times at this position to a depth of 1-$1^1/2$ inches (3-4 cm).

Check to see if the obstruction has come up into the child's mouth.

If this fails try again to breathe for the child, this time blowing harder to try to dislodge the obstruction or at least get air past it.

If this also fails, repeat the cycle of 5 backblows, 5 chest thrusts and mouth to mouth breathing until the airway clears or help arrives.

Check for circulation (C)

This is done at the carotid artery (p. 7) in the **child's neck.**

Slide your fingers into the groove alongside the windpipe. Press firmly to feel for the pulse.

Check the pulse for 5 seconds before deciding whether or not there is a pulse.

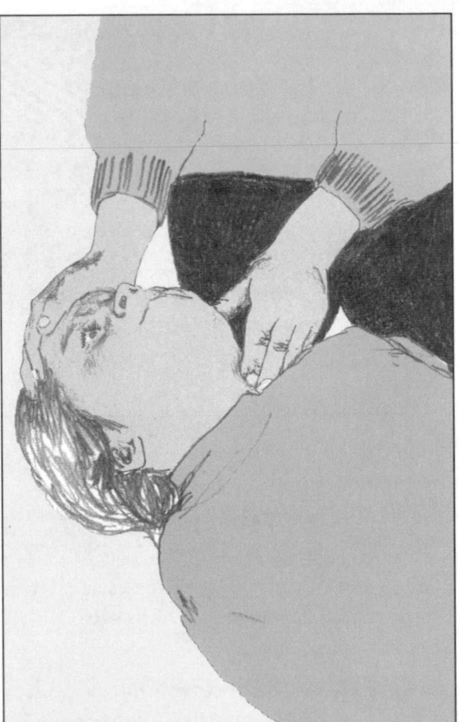

Chest Compressions for a Child

Place the child on a firm surface. Use the first and second fingers of one hand to find the position where the child's lower ribs meet the abdomen. Now slide your fingers up the line of the ribs to the notch where the ribs meet the breastbone. Place one finger in the notch and the other on the breastbone **next** to the first finger.

Place the heel of the other hand on to the breastbone immediately next to the fingers; this is where you will press down. Press in to a depth of $^{1}/_{2}$-1 in (1-3 cm) at a rate of 100 compressions per minute.

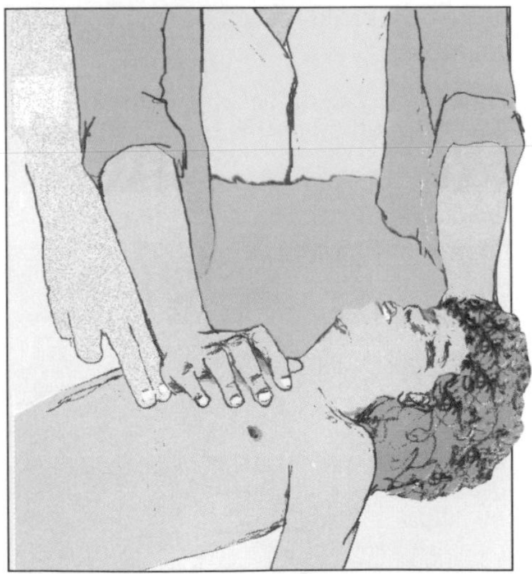

Sequence of Resuscitation

- Give 5 chest compressions to one breath (for one **or** two first aiders).

Recovery position for children

Unconscious children need to have their airways protected in the same way as for adults and babies.

For small children

Place the small child on his/her side with a rolled-up blanket (or similar) along the back; if necessary, tilt the head back very slightly so as to ensure an open airway.

Check the child's breathing at frequent intervals.

For older children

Before starting to put the child into the recovery position, remember to remove the child's glasses (if worn) and to remove any large articles from the pockets.

Kneel by the side of the child and gently tilt the head back. Straighten the legs so that turning is easier.

The child's arm closest to you is placed at a right angle to the body with the elbow bent so that the back of the hand lies flat against the ground. **Do not force** the hand on to the ground. You will need to find the position where this naturally occurs. For some, the arm may end up in a near 'saluting' position while, for others, the arm may be nearly straight.

Bring the other arm across the child's body so that the hand rests on the opposite shoulder. **Slide** your hand on to the upper part of that arm and do not let go, otherwise the arm will fall away.

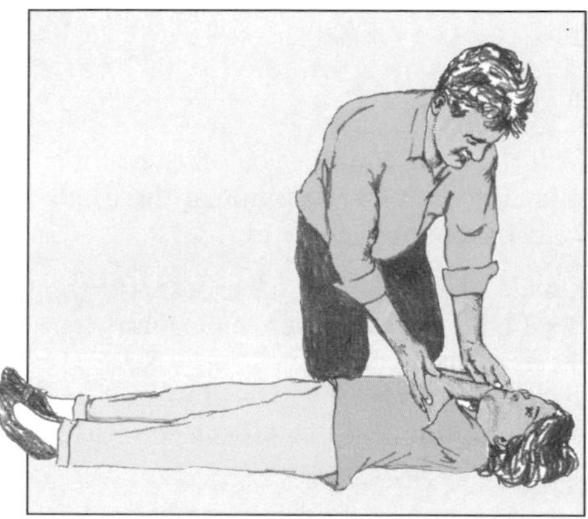

Using your free hand, grasp the child's outer thigh (just above the knee) on the leg further away from you. Pull the knee up until the foot on that leg rests alongside the child's other knee. Ensure that the foot is flat on the ground.

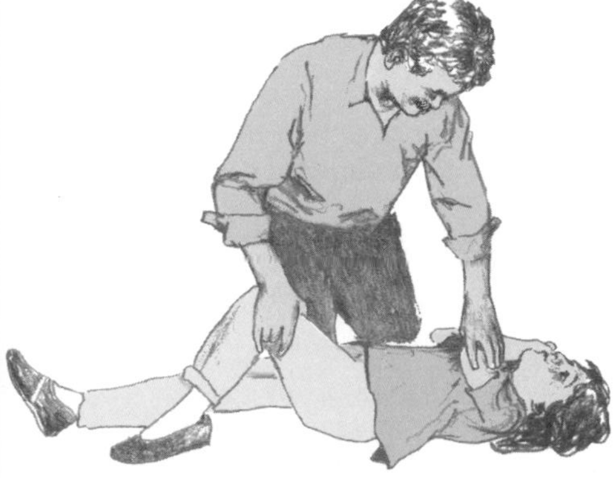

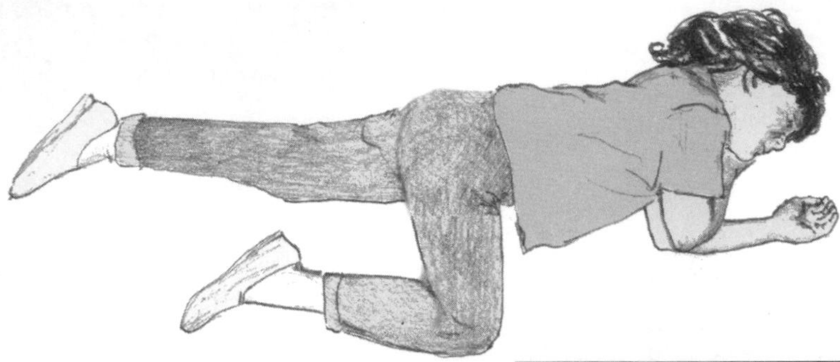

Roll the child towards you on to his/her side. This is done by pulling at the thigh whilst supporting the arm.

Once the child is on his/her side, tilt the head back so as to ensure a clear airway. If necessary, place one or both of the child's hands under the head so as to maintain this position. Check to see that the child is breathing.

Gently pull the child's upper leg so that it is at right angles at the hip and knee.

Check the child's breathing and pulse frequently while waiting for an ambulance to arrive.

1. If the child is already on his/her side then adjust the position so as to ensure an open airway and stability.
2. In the event of a chest injury, roll the child on to the **injured** side.
3. In the event of injured limbs that cannot be bent, use padding or bystanders to prevent the child from rolling face down.
4. If you have to leave an unconscious child alone, **always** leave him/her in the recovery position.

Spinal injuries

- If you suspect that an unconscious child may have a spinal injury then the priority is to ensure that he/she can breathe. If you are alone, turn the child gently into the recovery position. If you have someone to help, ask your assistant to support the child's head so that the head stays in line with the body during the turn and, once in position, use padding to supplement, but not replace the manual support (p. 134).

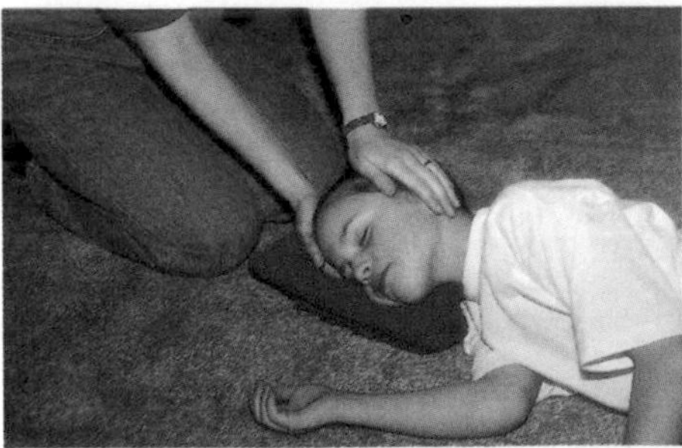

When to telephone for an ambulance

- If resuscitation is needed – after 1 minute of resuscitation.
- If unconscious – after placing the child in the recovery position.

Abdominal Pains

Abdominal pain, a relatively common complaint, can be trivial if due to indigestion, wind, etc., but may be serious when caused, for example, by a perforation in part of the bowel or by appendicitis. This is an area of first aid for which it is very difficult to give precise guidelines. Therefore common sense has to be used.

Colic

This type of pain is common with wind (causing distension of the bowel) or an obstruction in the bowel. It fluctuates in its severity and often causes periods of very severe pain.

You may notice • Periods of severe pain mingled with intervals of less severe pain or discomfort.

- Nausea and possibly vomiting.
- Cold sweats.
- Doubling-up with pain.

Treatment

Help the casualty to rest in the most comfortable position possible.

Place a hot water bottle with a cover or wrapped in a towel, or similar, on the casualty's abdomen.

If the pain is severe, the casualty collapses or the pain does not become easier within half an hour, seek medical advice.

Intense Pain

Intense pain that starts suddenly, remains fairly constant and is made worse by movement should always be regarded as potentially serious. It will be accompanied by a cold sweat, nausea and vomiting.

Treatment

Help the casualty to rest in the most comfortable possible position.

Place a covered hot water bottle on the casualty's abdomen.

Call for a doctor.

Indigestion

Indigestion can cause considerable discomfort. On occasions its onset is directly related to a recent meal; however, it may occur some considerable time after a meal, when the casualty lies flat or is awaiting a meal.

You may notice • Complaint of a 'burning' sensation up through the chest into the throat.

• A bilious taste in the mouth.

• Stomach feels uncomfortable and distended.

• Pain and discomfort in the upper abdomen and chest.

Treatment

Help the casualty to rest in a comfortable position.

Assist the casualty to take an indigestion remedy, if normally used.

If the discomfort has not eased after half an hour, seek medical advice.

Dial 999 for an ambulance

- If the casualty complains of indigestion with the pain/discomfort being present in the chest, the possibility of a heart attack must always be considered.
- If the chest pain/discomfort does not respond to the casualty's normal indigestion remedy, or is present for more than 5 minutes, dial 999 for an ambulance.

Aches and Pains

A variety of aches and pains affect us throughout our lives. Few require medical attention. Obviously, however, it is very important to be able to recognise when someone is in need of a doctor, rather than simple painkillers and rest.

When to see a doctor

There are few hard and fast rules in this respect; however, remember that it is often possible to ring your doctor's surgery (day or night) and to ask the doctor for advice, supplying pertinent facts such as how long the casualty has been ill, a resumé of symptoms and details of the body temperature.

As a guideline seek a doctor's opinion if any of the following are present:

- Headache associated with a raised temperature and neck stiffness.
- General malaise not improving after 48 hours.
- A raised temperature of 38°C (100.4°F) or more if the person feels unwell.
- A raised temperature of 39°C (102.2°F) whether or not unwell.
- Diarrhoea and vomiting that does not improve after 12 hours.
- Chest pain for longer than 5 minutes.

It must be emphasised that this list is not exhaustive and common sense has to be used when deciding to call a doctor. If you have any concerns **do not hesitate to seek medical advice.**

On occasions, when dealing with minor aches and pains, your local pharmacist will be able to advise.

Medication

Very often, aches and pains will benefit from simple painkillers such as paracetamol. Be sure to take any medication in strict accordance with the instructions on the packet/bottle. They will give you guidance on the quantity to be taken, at what intervals, and which precautions you should take in respect of alcohol, driving and operating machinery, etc.

If you are on regular medication you should ask the pharmacist to advise on suitable painkillers.

Remember that cough and cold remedies often contain measures of painkillers so exercise caution when taking other painkillers – ask your pharmacist.

Rest

Many common aches and pains respond well to rest, be it lying on the settee with a cup of tea or going to bed early.

Warmth

Applying warmth frequently over the area that aches provides relief. The easiest way to do this is to use a hot water bottle. Ensure that it has a cover or is wrapped in a towel (or similar).

For general aches and pains following physical exercise such as jogging, etc., a soak in a warm bath often provides relief.

Period Pain

For many women the few days just prior to and during the period can be uncomfortable, with cramps, lower abdominal pain and back pains.

Often the abdominal discomfort and pain is associated with other symptoms which may include mood changes, retention of fluid (swollen abdomen and ankles), nausea, general malaise, etc.

Treatment

Encourage the woman to rest in the most comfortable possible position.

A covered hot water bottle placed against the lower abdomen may give some relief.

Assist the woman to take her usual pain-killers if she has not already done so.

Medication

- Seek advice from your local pharmacy as to suitable simple remedies.
- If simple remedies are ineffective or if the quality of the woman's life is adversely affected, suggest she seeks medical advice.

Headache

A headache is a very common complaint and may accompany many illnesses, particularly those that include a fever such as flu. However, there are occasions when a headache accompanies more serious conditions such as meningitis or a stroke. The actual intensity of a headache can vary greatly from a feeling of 'heaviness' to 'blinding' pain.

Treatment

Help the casualty to rest in a quiet room.

The casualty may benefit from taking the recommended dose of a simple painkiller such as paracetamol or ibuprofen.

When to Seek Medical Advice

- If a severe headache develops very suddenly and incapacitates the casualty.
- If a headache is persistent or recurrent.
- If the casualty suffers drowsiness or a personality change.
- If the casualty complains of loss of muscle power or sensation.
- If the headache is accompanied by neck stiffness and a temperature.
- If the headache follows a head injury.
- If the headache persists for more than 2 hours.

Considerable relief may be achieved by darkening the room in which the casualty is resting.

Migraine Headache

This is a particularly severe and, at times, debilitating headache that often causes the casualty to feel unwell and may be accompanied by a wide variety of symptoms.

You may notice • Complaint of an intense headache, often restricted to one side of the head or behind the eyes.

• Accompanying visual disturbances, e.g. seeing bright lights or a 'blind' area.

• Intolerance of bright lights and noise.

• Nausea and vomiting.

Treatment

Take the casualty to a quiet room to rest.

Help to provide any migraine relief, such as tablets or a nasal spray.

Earache

Earache can be extremely distressing and may be caused by a variety of conditions, ranging from an infection within the middle ear to measles or a dental problem. Earache may be accompanied by temporary partial or complete deafness in the affected ear.

Treatment

Give the casualty the recommended dose of a simple painkiller such as paracetamol or ibuprofen.

Put a covered hot water bottle over the affected ear.

When to see a doctor

- ☐ If there is a fever.
- ☐ If there is a discharge from the ear.
- ☐ If the hearing loss is profound.

Earache during a flight

Due to the very rapid pressure changes within the ear during an aircraft flight, many people experience a period of earache. This is particularly likely to happen during take-off and before landing.

Treatment

Take frequent 'yawning' breaths once you feel the discomfort starting.

Chew gum or suck a sweet during take-off and descent.

If the pain is intense or does not settle, seek medical advice after landing.

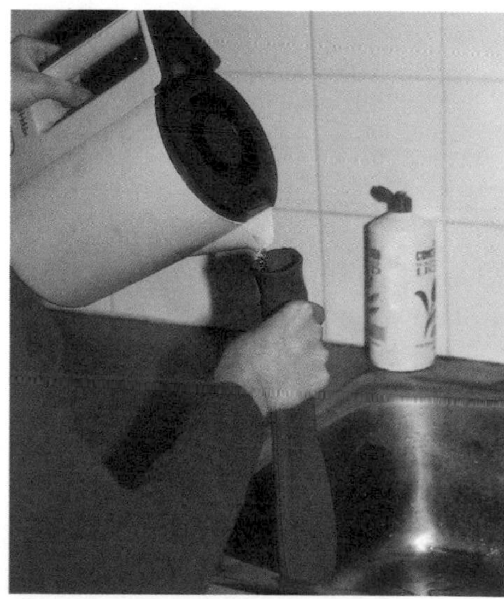

Allergies

Allergies are adverse reactions by the body to substances with which it comes in contact. These substances may be touched, swallowed, inhaled or injected. The allergy may exhibit itself in a number of ways; in some cases there may be more than one allergic response.

Types of allergic reaction

Respiratory allergies may result in asthma (p. 34) or hayfever. Causative agents of such allergies include pollen, dust, domestic pets, fumes, etc.

Intestinal allergies may result in abdominal pain/cramps, diarrhoea and vomiting. Causative agents of such allergies include food substances, drugs, etc.

Skin allergies may result in a rash or worsening of chronic dermatitis or eczema. Causes may be plants, domestic pets, foods, drugs, household chemicals, cleaners, etc.

Treatment

There is little a first aider can do to alleviate an allergic reaction beyond providing simple relief.

When to see a doctor

- If the allergy is causing discomfort or distress and the casualty cannot achieve symptomatic relief.
- If the casualty is **not** asthmatic and an asthma-like reaction occurs.
- Symptoms last for more than 48 hours after the source of the allergy has been removed.
- Swelling affects the face and/or neck.
- If the casualty becomes generally unwell, e.g. suffers a fever.
- If in doubt, seek medical advice.
- If the allergic response is mild and does not require a medical opinion it may be worth seeking advice from your local pharmacist.

Anaphylactic Shock

This is an allergic reaction that has a body-wide response. It is a serious condition that can prove fatal. Some people know that they are super-sensitive to certain things such as a particular drug, food or insect sting and may be carrying an antidote. Others will be unaware that they have developed this potentially life-threatening allergic response.

You may notice • Widespread body rash.

• Swelling, particularly of the face and neck.

• Distress.

• Profound anxiety.

• A fast pulse.

- Feeling of a 'tight chest'.
- Difficulty in breathing.
- Collapse and unconsciousness.

Treatment

If the casualty carries an antidote, help to administer it as a priority.

Dial 999 for an ambulance.

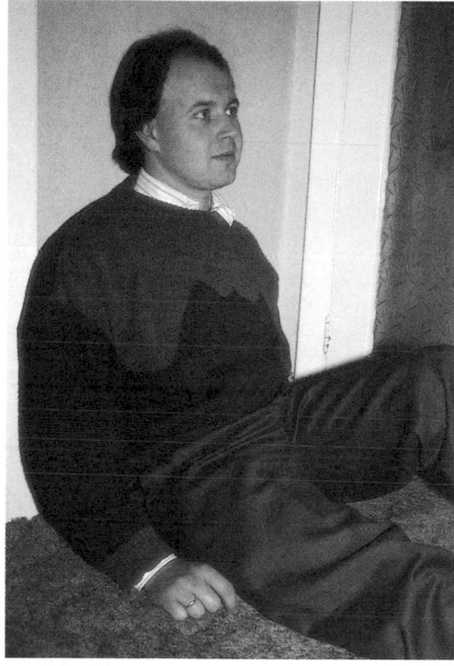

Help the casualty to rest in the most comfortable sitting position.

If the casualty becomes unconscious, check the ABC of Resuscitation and treat as appropriate (p. 6).

Hayfever

This is an uncomfortable reaction to pollen which causes a runny nose, swollen, itchy eyes and other symptoms resembling a head cold.

Treatment

Seek advice from a pharmacist.

If the symptoms are severe, seek medical advice.

Skin Rashes

Skin rashes can be extremely irritating and cause considerable discomfort.

Treatment

Advise the casualty not to scratch the rash.

Apply a cold compress or calamine lotion.

If the distress caused by the rash is severe, or the rash persists for more than 24 hours, seek medical advice.

If the rash is possibly due to prescribed medication, ***do not*** stop taking it without seeking medical advice.

See also **Skin Rashes,** p. 131.

Ambulance Service

For anyone who has been in an accident or is unwell and needs to go to hospital urgently, an ambulance is the best means of travel.

Help at hand

The ambulance crew are highly trained and skilled professionals who will start effective treatment at the scene and continue it throughout the journey to hospital. Increasingly today at least one member of the crew will be a paramedic who can perform advanced life-saving procedures. The advent of paramedic care has been a major factor in improving the outcome for victims of accidents and sudden illness.

The ambulance carries a wide variety of equipment and allows the casualty to be transported either lying down or sitting up, whichever is more comfortable.

Sudden emergencies

Wherever they occur, sudden emergencies often require an ambulance rather than a doctor.

In an emergency, dial 999 and ask for the ambulance service. Tell the operator your telephone number and location and give a brief description of the emergency (including the number of casualties). Answer the questions clearly and calmly.

Do not forget to mention any landmarks that will make finding you easier and, where possible, arrange for someone to meet the ambulance. Do not hang up until the ambulance service have done so.

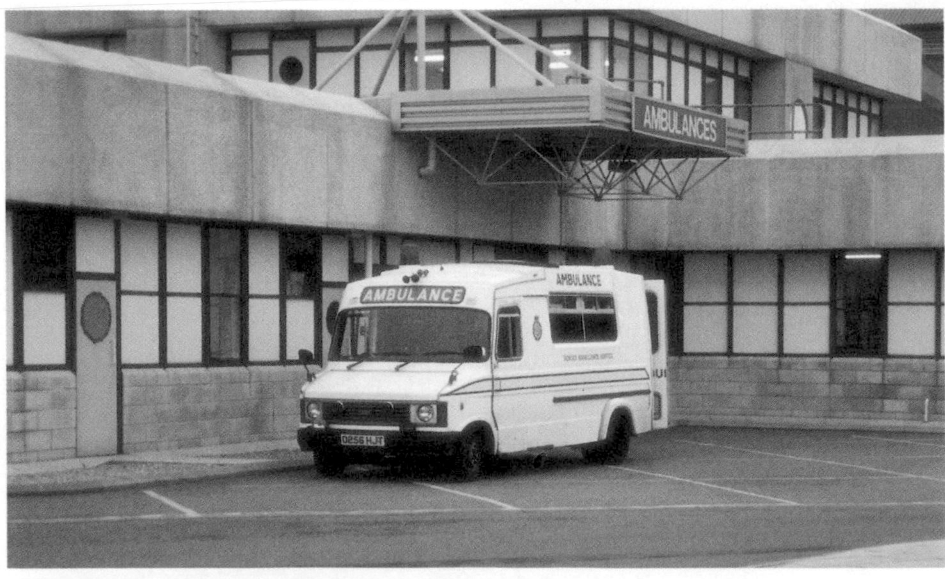

Amputation

Amputation is the total separation of a part of the body during an accident. With the advent of micro-surgery, it is possible to sew severed parts back on and for many people to gain near normal movement and sensation. However, unless the right steps are taken immediately following the accident, successful surgery is less likely.

Priorities

- Stop bleeding.
- Treat shock.
- Preserve the amputated part.

Stop bleeding

As with any wound, the stump will be bleeding because blood vessels will have been severed. In the case of fingers and toes, the bleeding is not going to be immediately life-threatening but when hands, feet and other limbs are amputated, there will certainly be very serious bleeding (both venous and arterial).

Put direct pressure on to the bleeding stump.

Elevate the remaining part of the limb.

Put a sterile dressing on the stump (see p. 42) and remember to keep the limb elevated.

> If there is a clean amputation through a guillotine or similar implement, the initial bleeding may not be too serious. However, after a few minutes more serious arterial bleeding (spurts of bright red blood) may start.

Treat shock

As with any accident, shock will be present. If the bleeding is severe, the effects of shock can threaten the casualty's life.

Lie the casualty down with legs raised.

Protect the casualty from the cold.

Elevate the remaining part of the limb.

Preserve the amputated part

Put the amputated part into a plastic bag and seal it.

Pad the bag with soft fabric, e.g. a towel.

Place the padded part in another container that contains crushed ice.

Send to hospital with the casualty.

1. ***Do not*** place the amputated part in direct contact with the ice.
2. If ice is not available, use a pack of frozen vegetables instead.

Treatment Summary

Stop the bleeding by techniques such as direct pressure on the wound, elevating the part and applying a pressure dressing. Treat for shock as above.

Asthma

Asthma is a condition that makes breathing out difficult. It affects the air passages in the lungs and can be triggered by a variety of causes including allergy, stress or smoke.
Often, however, there is no obvious cause to the asthma attack. Attacks are sudden and can be alarming, both to the casualty and onlookers. Many asthmatics carry medication which they take during an asthma attack. Usually, this is taken as an inhaler.

Recognising asthma

You will notice • Difficulty with breathing (particularly breathing out).

You may notice • A wheezing sound on breathing out.

• Increased breathing rate.

• Increased pulse rate.

• Speaking in single words or short sentences.

• Increasing anxiety and restlessness.

If the attack is very severe or prolonged, the casualty will become very tired and, in extreme cases, he/she collapses into unconsciousness.

TREATMENT

Help the casualty to sit down and lean forward on to a table or similar support. It may be more comfortable.

Wherever possible, provide fresh air for the casualty.

Assist the casualty to use his/her inhaler.

Loosen any tight clothing.

Encourage the casualty to keep calm and to take even breaths.

When to call for help

Frequent sufferers of asthma attacks will often manage their own treatment and require little or no assistance. However, those who are not familiar with their condition or who, for some reason, have a more serious attack than usual, will generally require medical help.

If the casualty is exhausted or at the point of collapse, send for an ambulance without delay: this also applies if breathing is very distressed. For less serious attacks, be guided by the casualty. If you call for medical assistance, wait for the doctor in case the casualty becomes worse.

In the event of an asthma attack in the street or away from home, call for an ambulance rather than letting the casualty return home to call his/her doctor.

CALL AN AMBULANCE

- ☐ If the casualty is exhausted.
- ☐ If the casualty's usual medication does not work.
- ☐ If the casualty's breathing is very distressed.
- ☐ If you cannot contact the casualty's doctor (e.g. when away from home).

Back Problems

The term 'back problems' can apply to a wide variety of conditions. For convenience, these may be categorised as strains, lifting injuries and whiplash injuries.

Back Strain

This is a very common condition caused by over-exerting the muscles that surround the spinal column and is often made worse by poor posture. The most common sites affected are the lower or small of the back and the neck.

You may notice • Complaints of general aching in the area affected.

• Increased discomfort when using the back muscles, particularly with leaning forward and twisting actions.

• Often this type of back problem is recurrent and, apart from providing relief from the worst of the discomfort, there is little that the first aider can do.

Treatment

In severe cases:

Help the casualty to lie down in the most comfortable position.

Give simple painkillers such as paracetamol or ibuprofen. Remember to read the instructions on the packaging of the drug.

Apply a hot water bottle (with a cover or wrapped in a towel) to the affected area.

If the discomfort has not greatly diminished after 1 hour, seek medical advice.

In less severe cases:

Help the casualty to rest in the most comfortable position – usually lying flat.

Apply a hot water bottle (with a cover or wrapped in a towel) to the affected area.

Give simple painkillers.

When to Call a Doctor

- If the casualty's back has 'locked'.
- If the pain is very severe.
- If painkillers and rest do not provide relief within 6 hours.

A casualty who is experiencing recurrent back problems, even of a minor nature, should be encouraged to make an appointment to see the doctor.

Lifting Injuries

Lifting injuries, regrettably, are very common. Often there is a history of recurrent back problems. However, injuries caused by lifting tend to be more distressing than recurrent back strain and in a significant number of cases are likely to cause increased damage to the back.

In severe cases you will notice
• Excruciating pain and discomfort.

• Restricted movement – tendency to walk slowly, stoop and hold the back.

You may also notice • 'Locked' back – inability to move from one position.

• Complaint of feeling the back 'go'.

In less severe cases you are dealing with a back strain (see p. 35).

TREATMENT

In severe cases:

Help the casualty to rest as comfortably as possible. If in a 'locked position', seat the casualty on a firm chair.

Call for assistance. It is usually advisable to call for an ambulance; however, failing this, **always** seek medical advice.

In less severe cases treat as for back strain (see p. 35).

Whiplash Injuries

Frequently, following minor road accidents, a casualty will complain of neck stiffness becoming worse over a matter of hours. This is usually referred to as a 'whiplash' injury. The sudden flicking of the head backward and forward during the accident causes an overstretching of the muscles around the cervical (neck) spine, and they go into a painful spasm.

Should you come across an accident involving a potential injury to the neck, it is most important to treat it as a spinal injury (p. 132) rather than assuming that the casualty has a less serious whiplash injury.

You will notice • Complaint of neck stiffness and discomfort that becomes progressively more severe.

You may notice • Head and neck held in one position.

• Complaint of tingling in the arms.

TREATMENT

Help the casualty to support the head and neck in a comfortable position.

Seek medical advice.

If you have any concern that the casualty may have sustained a spinal injury (p. 132), **treat it as such without delay.**

Complications

When certain other symptoms accompany back (or neck) pain, medical advice should always be sought without any delay. These are:

- Fever.
- Headache.
- Nausea.
- Vomiting.
- Altered sensation in part of the body.
- Drowsiness or loss of consciousness.
- Incontinence.

Bandages and Dressings

Bandaging is a useful skill for the first aider. Bandages can be used to hold dressings in place, to control bleeding, to support injuries, to immobilise injuries and to reduce swelling.

There are four main types of bandage:

Triangular bandages.

Roller bandages.

Sterile dressings.

Tubular gauze.

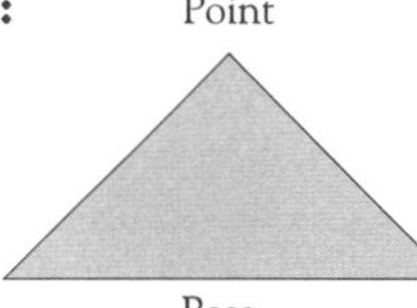

The longest edge of a triangular bandage is called its base. The corner opposite is known as its point.

Triangular bandages

These have a number of uses.

Slings: to support arm injuries.

Pads: when other dressing material is not available, or for the comfort of the casualty.

Folded: to use as a bandage to hold a pad in place or to immobilise injured limbs.

Broad arm sling

USE FOR:

- Fractured forearm and wrist.
- Fractured upper arm.
- Fractured shoulder-blade.
- Dislocated shoulder.
- Fractured elbow (if it can be bent).

Ensure that the injured arm is supported throughout.

Tuck the bandage between the casualty's arm and chest with the **point** under the elbow on the injured arm.

Pass the upper end of the bandage around the back of the casualty's neck from the uninjured to the injured side.

Bring up the lower end (enclosing the casualty's forearm) so that the two ends meet at the shoulder on the injured side.

Tie a reef knot at the hollow above the collar bone on the injured side.

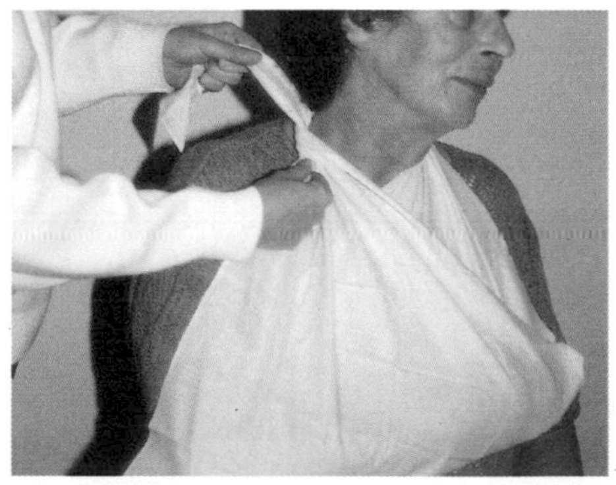

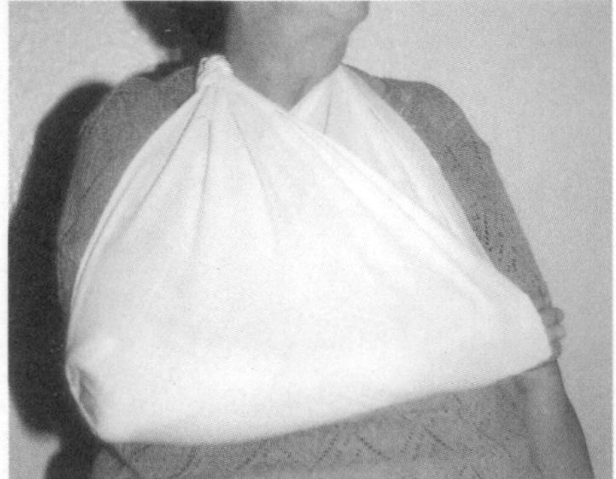

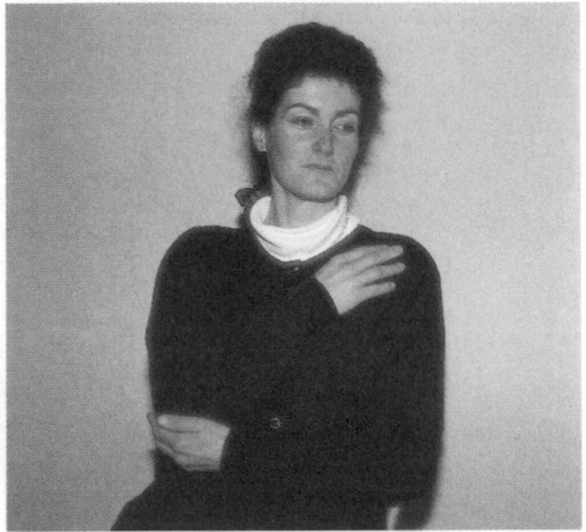

Secure the point of the bandage by a safety pin or similar fixing at the front of the elbow.

Alternatively, twist the point round and round until the bandage fits snugly around the elbow, but is not too tight and causing restriction. Then tuck the twisted end firmly into the sling at the front.

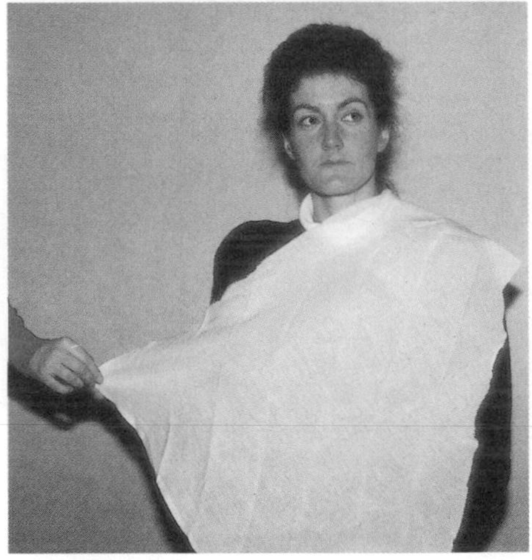

Elevation sling

USE FOR:

- Hand injuries (including serious cuts).
- Elevation of forearm for serious cuts.
- Fractured collar bone.

Place the injured arm across casualty's chest with fingertips on opposite shoulder.

Ensure that the injured arm is supported in this position.

Place the triangular bandage **over** the affected arm with the **point** over the elbow and the upper end tucked over the shoulder on the unaffected side.

Tuck the base of the bandage under the forearm so that the forearm is enclosed from the fingertips to the elbow.

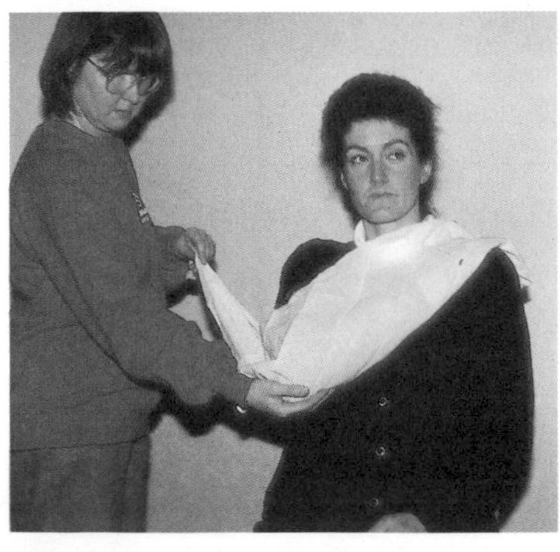

Bring the lower **end** of the bandage up across the casualty's back to meet the other end at the unaffected shoulder.

Tie the ends together in the hollow above the casualty's collar bone on the uninjured side.

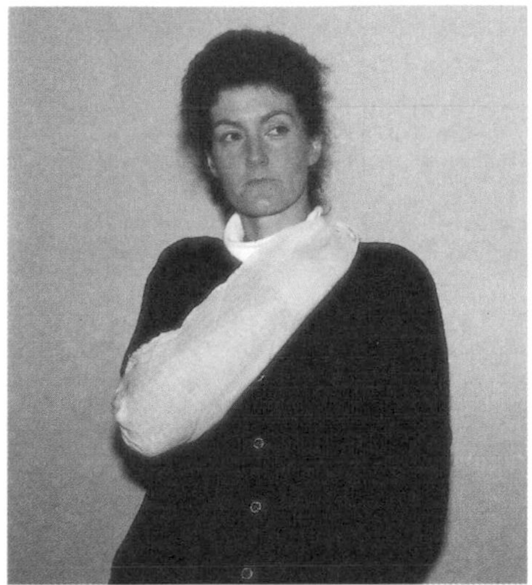

Secure the point by a safety pin at the front of the elbow. Alternatively, twist the point round and round until the bandage fits snugly around the elbow; tuck the point into the sling at the front.

Improvising slings

Broad arm sling: Fold the casualty's shirt/jumper up and over the injured forearm and pin it to the front of itself.

Elevation sling: Use a belt, tie or similar to support the arm. ***Do not* use this if you suspect a fracture to the forearm.**

Other uses for a triangular bandage

The triangular bandage can also be used to provide a light covering for knee, hand/foot or scalp injuries. All of these bandages will hold a pad or dressing in place but will not exert enough pressure to be of any use for stopping serious bleeding. Additionally, triangular bandages can be used to immobilise a limb.

Immobilising a limb

This technique is used when you are unable to effectively immobilise a lower limb just using your hands and rolled-up blankets/towels, etc., or when the arrival of the ambulance is likely to be delayed.

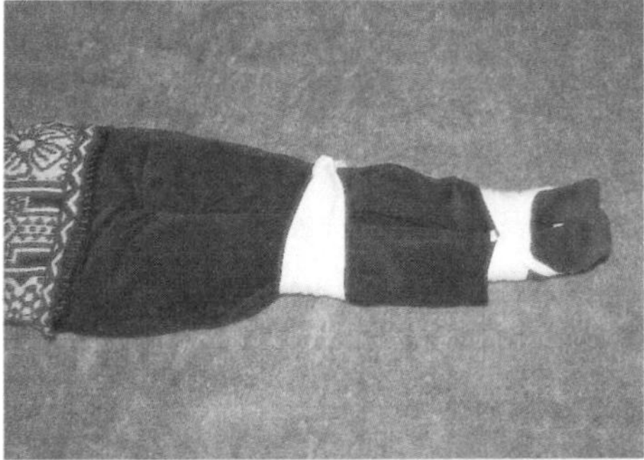

Place soft padding between the casualty's limbs, particular attention being paid to the knees and ankles. Clothing, towels or folded triangular bandages all make suitable soft padding.

The knees are enclosed in a **broad-fold** triangular bandage, while the ankles are enclosed in a **narrow-fold** bandage.

Broad-fold triangular bandage

Fold the point of the triangular bandage horizontally so that it touches the base.

Fold the bandage in half again to make the broad-fold triangular bandage.

Narrow-fold triangular bandage

Fold the bandage into a broad-fold bandage.

Fold the bandage in half again to make the narrow-fold triangular bandage.

Roller bandages

These are used to give support to sprains and strains, to hold dressings in place and to control bleeding. The commonest types available are:

Open weave: non-elasticated, to hold dressings in place.

Conforming: lightly elasticated, to hold dressings in place, to control bleeding and to give light support to sprains and strains.

Crepe: elasticated, to provide firm support to sprains and strains.

Be sure to use the most appropriate type of roller bandage for the task and choose an appropriate size according to the chart below.

SIZING A ROLLER BANDAGE

- Leg: 4-6 in (10-15 cm) width
- Arm: 3-4 in (7.5-10 cm) width
- Hand: 2-3 in (5-7.5 cm) width

Securing a roller bandage

There are four methods:

(i) Tying off: after applying the bandage cut down the middle of the loose end for 8-10 in (20-25 cm). Tie a knot at the bottom of the cut using both sides of the cut bandage. Pass the ends around the limb, one in each direction, and tie the two ends together (preferably with a reef knot).

(ii) Safety pins: often supplied with the bandage.

(iii) Adhesive tape.

(iv) Bandage clips: may be supplied with the bandage.

Check the circulation once you have secured the bandage.

Do this by pressing on to one of the casualty's nails on the hand/foot of the injured limb. The nail bed will become very pale. When you release the pressure the colour should quickly return. If the colour does not return or takes more than 2-3 seconds, loosen the bandage just enough to achieve normal circulation. Retest the circulation after tying off the bandage.

Rules for roller bandages

Bandage from the inside outwards (i.e. from the inner surface of the limb out towards you). When the affected part is between two joints, always start just above the joint **below** the injury and finish and bandage just below the joint **above** the injury.

Do not over-stretch the bandage as this may cut off the circulation.

Leave the finger tips or toes unbandaged so that you can check the circulation.

Never tie off a bandage midway up a limb.

Recheck the circulation frequently in case swelling tightens the bandage.

Bandaging techniques

Along a limb

Start just above the joint below the injury. Make two straight turns around the limb, working from the inside outwards.

Start to 'spiral' the bandage up the limb; each layer should cover a half to three-quarters of the previous layer.

Finish the bandage just below the joint above the injury. Do this by making one or two straight turns around the limb and

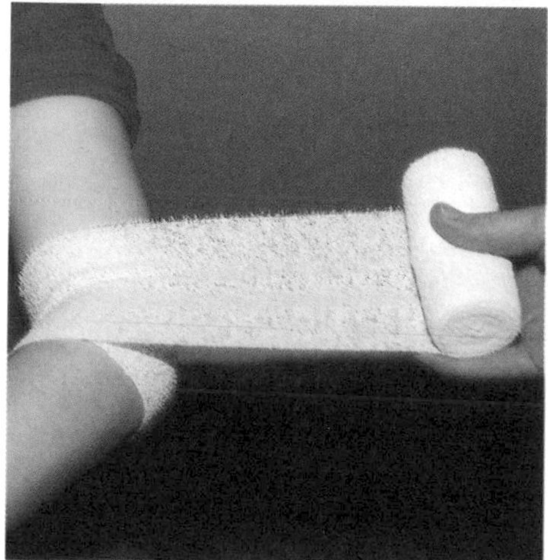

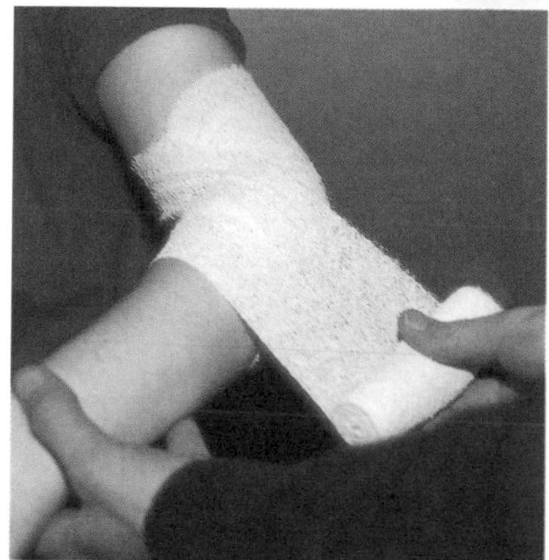

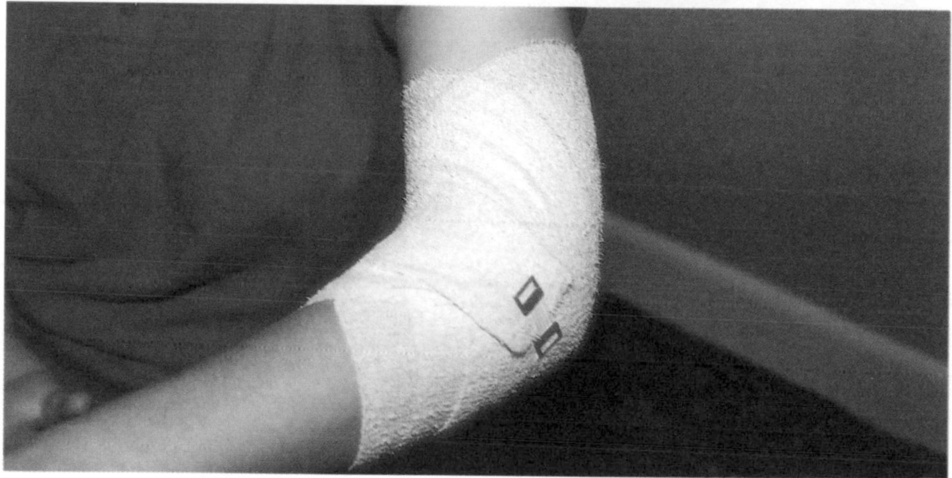

then secure it. If necessary, cut off any excess bandage.

Check the circulation in the fingers or toes on the bandaged limb.

Around the knee or elbow

The injured knee or elbow should be moved into a slightly bent position. Wrap the bandage around the elbow two times so that the joint is covered. Remember to work from the inside of the limb outward.

Make one turn around the upper limb and now cross over the crease of the joint so as to make one turn around the lower limb.

Continue this, alternating the turns between the upper and lower limb. Do not allow the bandage to extend beyond one or two bandage widths on either side of the joint.

Finish with two straight turns and secure the bandage.

Check the circulation.

Around the wrist or ankle

Make two straight turns around the injured wrist or ankle. Remember to work from the inside of the limb outward.

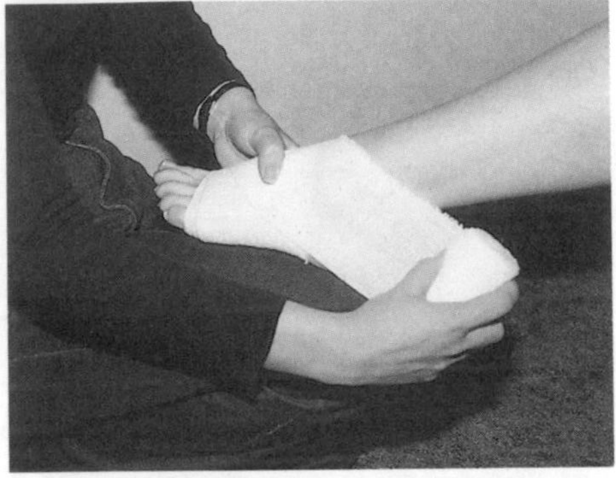

Take the bandage across the hand or foot and around it once, enclosing the fingers or toes but not the finger tips/toe ends. (In the case of a wrist bandage, the thumb is kept free – bandage around it).

Take the bandage back down around the wrist/ankle.

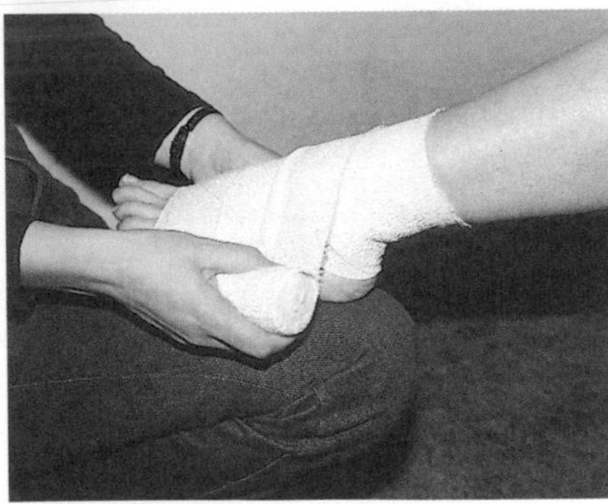

Bandage alternately with one turn across and around the hand/foot and then one around the wrist/ankle. On each sequence of turns around the hand/foot, bring the body of the bandage closer to the wrist/ankle.

Extend the bandage no more than one bandage width above the wrist/ankle.

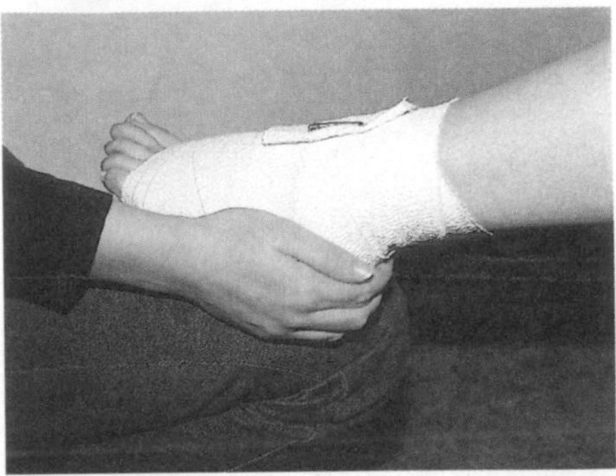

Finish with two straight turns around the wrist/ankle and secure the bandage.

Check the circulation on a finger/toe of the injured limb.

Sterile dressings

These are also known as 'shell' dressings and 'ambulance' dressings, consisting of a pre-packed pad attached to a roller bandage. They are used for covering wounds and to control bleeding.

Open the packet carefully so as not to let the pad and bandage unravel.

Unwind the loose end of the bandage; unfold the sterile pad, taking care not to contaminate it with your fingers.

Hold the bandage on either side of the pad and place the pad on the wound.

Take the shorter end of the bandage around the pad for two turns of the limb in order to anchor the dressing and bandage it in place.

Using the main body of the bandage, secure the whole pad to the wound with a simple spiralling bandage technique. (You will need to leave the short end of the bandage free.)

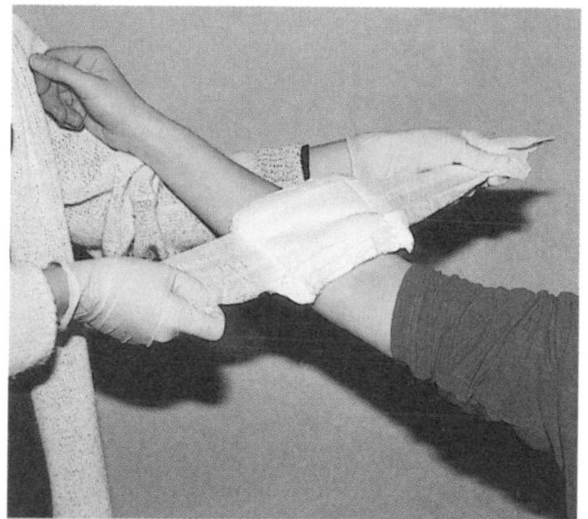

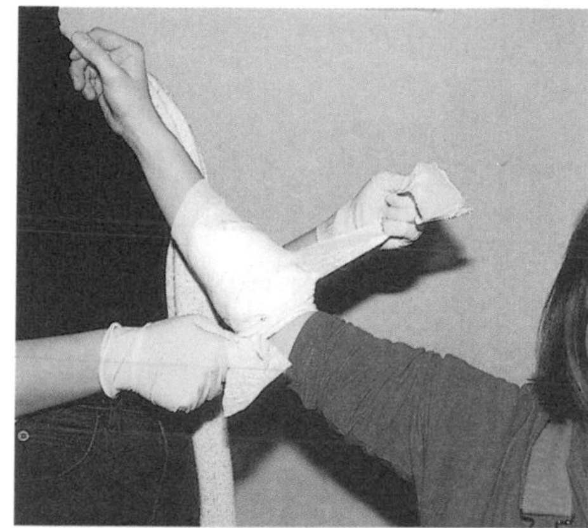

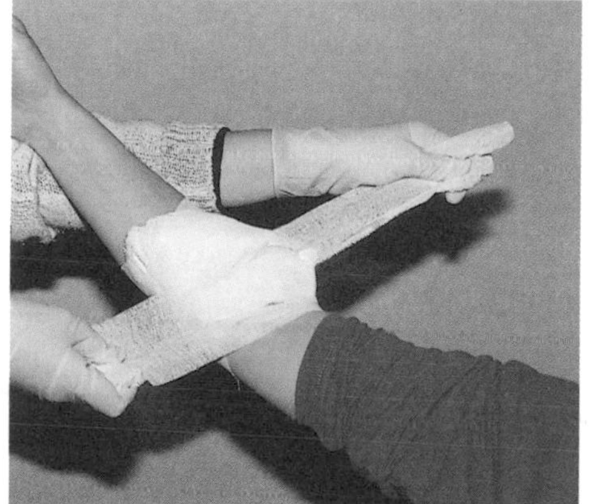

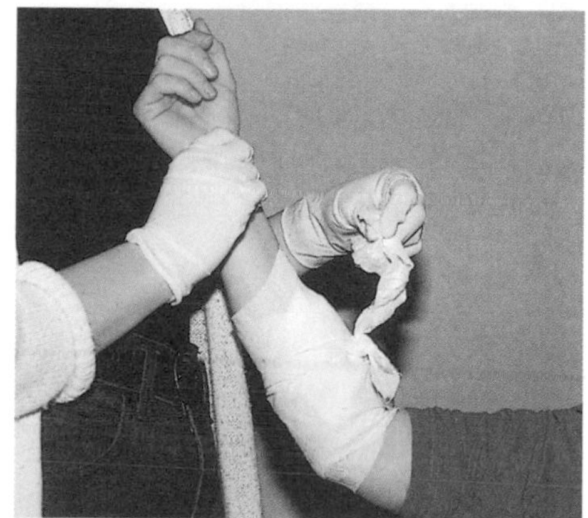

Take the short end of the bandage and make one turn around the limb in the opposite direction to flow of the main bandage.

Tie the two ends of the bandage together (preferably with a reef knot) over the pad so as to exert pressure on the wound.

Check the circulation on a finger/toe of the injured limb.

> If blood soaks through the sterile dressing, *do not* remove it. Bandage a further sterile dressing over the first. Do this as often as necessary until the bleeding stops.

Tubular gauze

This is a lightly elasticated tubular bandage made of seamless gauze. It is used for holding dressings in place on fingers and toes. It must not be used as a method of controlling bleeding. Care is needed to ensure that the circulation to the finger/toe is not impaired. A special applicator is needed and is provided on purchase of the roll.

Cut a piece of tubular gauze approximately 2-3 times the length of the finger/toe to be bandaged.

Push the whole length of the tubular gauze on to the applicator.

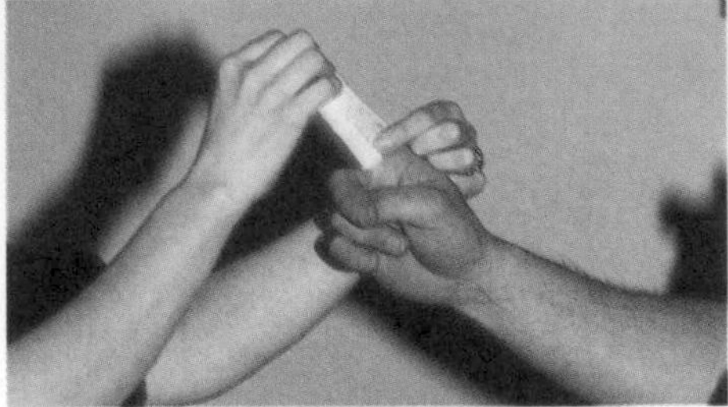

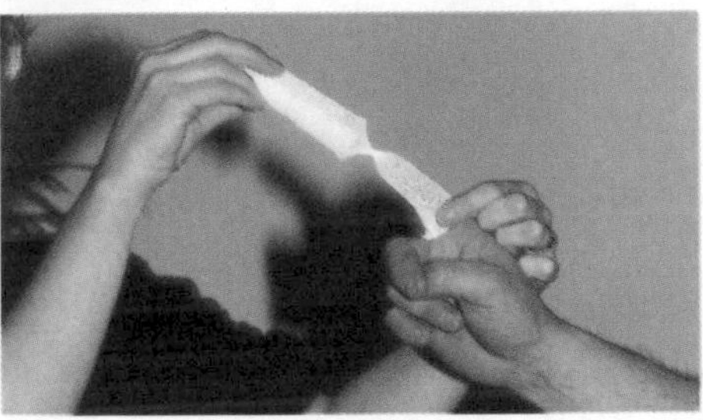

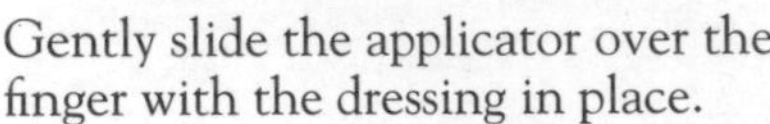

Gently slide the applicator over the finger with the dressing in place.

Hold the base of the tubular gauze in place and slowly withdraw the applicator to just beyond the end of the finger/toe.

Twist the applicator twice.

Gently push the applicator back down over the first layer of tubular gauze.

Remove the applicator, leaving the second layer of tubular gauze in place.

Secure with a piece of adhesive tape but do not completely encircle the finger as this may cut off the circulation.

Plasters

These are extremely useful for small wounds. They come in a variety of shapes and sizes and are made up of a small pad attached to an adhesive strap. Specially shaped plasters are available for use on fingertips, heels, etc.; these are usually butterfly-shaped with a central dressing. Some plasters are waterproof and these should be used on fingers and hands.

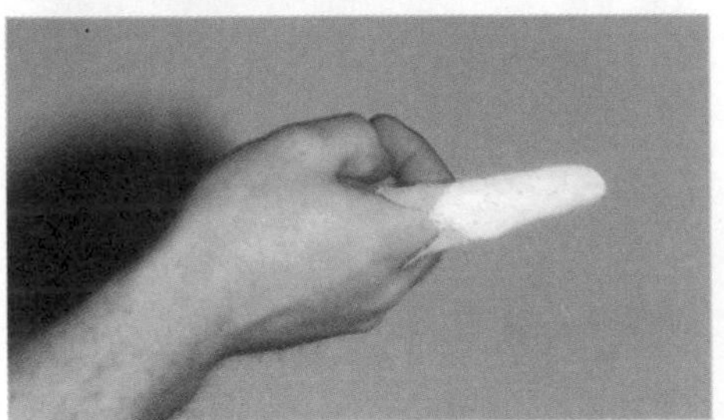

How to put on a plaster

Clean the wound under running water and dry, or use an antiseptic wipe and allow the skin to dry.

Choose a plaster of the right shape and size for the wound.

Hold the plaster by the protective strips and peel them back. ***Do not*** completely remove the protective strips.

Put the pad directly on to the wound and pull away the protective strips completely so that the adhesive strip makes contact with the casualty's skin.

Smooth the adhesive strip down.

> For finger/toe tips, elbows and heels, use specially shaped plasters. The wings of the plaster are individually smoothed into place so that the plaster fits properly and stays in place.

Food handlers must wear blue plasters to cover cuts, grazes, etc. on their hands and fingers.

Bites and Stings

Fortunately, many bites and stings are minor and, although irritating, respond well to simple first aid. Bites from humans and animals may be more serious. Because their mouths harbour many germs that can cause infection, these wounds always require medical attention. Snake bites pose a problem due to the venom that may be injected.

Insect Stings

Initially, many insect stings are painful but rarely present any danger to life. Occasionally, someone may be allergic to particular insect stings and suffer a more serious reaction. In more extreme cases, this may be a super-sensitive reaction called anaphylactic shock (p. 30) which can be fatal.

Treatment

Remove any sting left in the skin. Use a pair of tweezers. Ensure that you grip the sting below the poison sac so as not to inject further poison into the casualty.

Apply a cold compress to the area for at least 10-15 minutes.

If reaction is severe or irritation persists beyond 48 hours, seek medical advice.

Stings in the Mouth or Throat

- The resultant swelling can cause partial or complete obstruction of the casualty's airway.
- Stings in and around the mouth can be fatal and should always be treated as an emergency.

Treating a Sting in the Mouth

- Give the casualty ice to suck.
- Dial 999 for an ambulance.
- Keep the casualty calm and discourage crying or speaking as this may increase the swelling.
- Monitor the casualty for any signs of breathing difficulties.

Sea Creature Stings

The greater number of marine creatures that live around Britain's shores do not carry a sting. Those that do can inflict a very uncomfortable sting but pose little danger to life.

Treatment

Apply a compress to the area using a towel or similar soaked in alcohol or vinegar. Do this for 5 minutes.

Make up a paste of water and soda bicarbonate powder (equal parts of each) and apply to the affected area. Leave for 5 minutes.

Dust talcum powder over the affected area.

This recipe will neutralise any 'live' stinging cells left on the surface of the skin and thus reduce the effects of the injury.

If the area remains very painful, apply a cold compress and reassess the situation after 15-20 minutes.

Refer to a doctor if the area remains very painful or if the swelling becomes severe.

In severe cases

If the casualty complains of any breathing difficulties, i.e. tight chest or shortness of breath, dial 999 for an ambulance without delay.

Puncture wounds from marine creatures

Some marine creatures such as the weaver fish inject the venom through a puncture wound.

Treatment

Immerse the injured area in hot water for 20-30 minutes. The water should be as hot as the casualty can tolerate.

If the area remains very painful or is badly swollen, send the casualty to hospital. ***Do not*** try to remove any spines left embedded in the skin – they need to be removed under medical supervision.

Animal and Human Bites

Potentially, bites from animals (and humans) can leave very nasty wounds. The teeth carry infection into the tissues and **any** bite that punctures the skin **always** needs to be seen by a doctor. Human bites cause problems due to the crushing of underlying tissues which often is not visible to the first aider.

Rabies

While not a problem in Britain, animal bites inflicted when abroad may transmit rabies. This is a viral infection that affects the nervous system and may be fatal.

Do not approach any animal that shows a fear of water, or is acting in an irrational or aggressive manner.

If you are bitten, seek medical help. Report the incident to your medical insurance company.

Treatment for Bites

For a serious wound

Control serious bleeding by direct pressure and, if possible, by elevating the injured part (p. 48).

Apply a sterile dressing (p. 42).

Send the casualty to hospital.

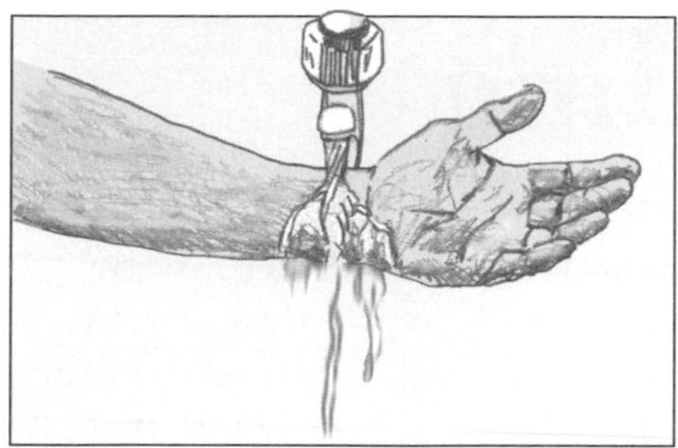

For a minor wound

Rinse the wound under running water for at least 5 minutes.

Wash the wound with soap and warm water.

Dry the wound and surrounding area.

Apply a suitable dressing (p. 37).

Advise the casualty to seek medical advice.

Snake Bites

The adder (viper) is Britain's only native snake whose bite is venomous. However, its effects are rarely fatal. Other snakes may be encountered when abroad. Very occasionally an exotic snake kept as a pet may bite someone and inflict a more serious, though rarely fatal, injury.

You may notice • A pair of puncture marks.

- Pain and discomfort around the site of the bite.
- Swelling and redness around the site of the bite.
- Breathing difficulties.
- Drowsiness.
- Vomiting.
- Visual problems.
- Excessive sweating.

Treatment

Keep the casualty calm and lay him/her down.

Wash the wound with soap and water, if possible.

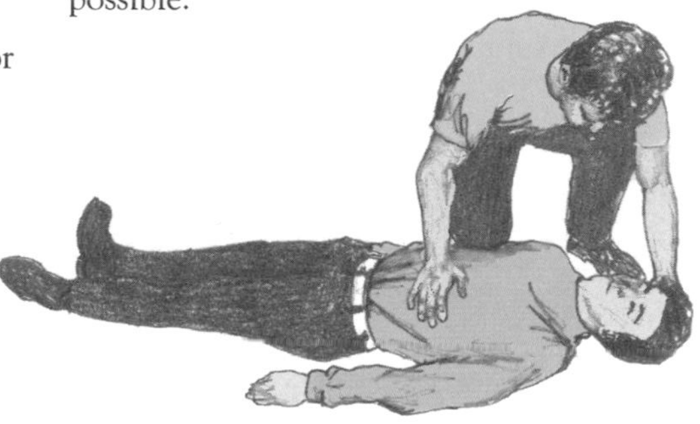

Keep the wound below the level of the heart so that the effects of the venom remain localised.

Dial 999 for an ambulance.

Immobilise the affected part if the casualty becomes restless.

Dos and Don'ts

- ☐ ***Do not*** apply a tourniquet.
- ☐ ***Do not*** attempt to suck out the venom.
- ☐ ***Do not*** open the wound with a knife 'to release the poison'.

DO TRY TO IDENTIFY THE SNAKE. NOTE ITS COLOURING AND PATTERN OF MARKINGS.

REMEMBER!
SNAKES RARELY ATTACK WITHOUT PROVOCATION.

Bleeding

Blood is essential to life and is normally contained within the circulatory system: the heart, arteries, capillaries and veins. When these are torn or damaged, bleeding occurs. This can be on the outside of the body through a visible wound or on the inside of the body (internal bleeding). Blood carries oxygen from the lungs to the heart along the arteries to the tissues, and through the tissues in the capillaries where the oxygen is made available for use. Veins carry the deoxygenated blood back to the heart.

Types of bleeding

Bleeding is classified according to the blood vessel that has been damaged. This may be identified by observing the colour and flow of the blood.

Arterial

Bright red blood that rhythmically spurts from the body in time with the heart beating. This is very serious bleeding and can rapidly lead to collapse and death.

Venous

Dark red blood that may ooze from a wound. If a large vein is damaged the oozing is copious and can rapidly lead to collapse and death.

Capillary

This is the trickling of blood seen with minor cuts and wounds. It is not serious.

Serious bleeding

This is bleeding that is extremely profuse and may be arterial (bright red blood) or venous (dark red blood). You will notice large amounts of blood on and around the casualty.

Treatment

If the casualty is unconscious, remember the ABC of Resuscitation (p. 6).

Put direct pressure with your hands on to the wound. If it is possible, do this using a sterile or clean pad – but **do not** waste time looking for first aid materials.

> If there is something sticking out of the wound, press down firmly on either side of the protrusion without dislodging it and bandage around.

Lay the casualty down.

Raise the injured part above the level of the casualty's heart.

As soon as a first aid kit is available, apply a sterile dressing (p. 42).

Keep the limb elevated, using an elevation sling for forearm and hand wounds.

Dial 999 for an ambulance.
Treat the casualty for shock (p. 129).

Check the dressing frequently to ensure that the bleeding is controlled.

Serious bleeding that will not stop

Do not remove the original dressing. Apply further sterile dressings over the original one.

Continue to apply direct pressure and maintain the limb elevation.

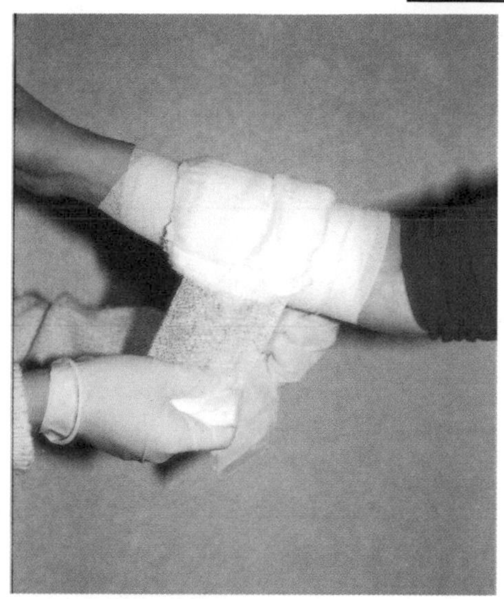

TOURNIQUETS

- ☐ ***Do not*** use a tourniquet – it can cause severe damage to the limb and can make the bleeding worse.

Site of bleeding	Type of bleeding	Cause
NOSE/EAR	Thin, watery blood loss	Escape of cerebro-spinal fluid (p. 111).
MOUTH	Frothy, bright red blood that is coughed up	Bleeding in the lungs
	Altered blood that is vomited up and looks like coffee grounds	Bleeding in the upper gut/stomach
	Fresh blood	Bitten tongue or lip
ANUS	Fresh blood	Maybe piles or a bleed from within the lower bowel
	Digested blood passed as a black, sticky stool with a strong offensive odour	Bleeding from the upper part of the gut
VAGINA	Heavy bleed when a period is not expected	Possible miscarriage/injury to the womb or vagina
URETHRA	Bloodstained urine	Bleeding within the urinary system. Possible kidney injury/infection

Obviously, if any of these symptoms occur, medical advice needs to be sought. If the casualty has signs of an internal bleed or shock (p. 51), an ambulance should be called immediately.

Less serious bleeding

Where the bleeding is not profuse and life is not endangered, the same principles still apply.

Apply direct pressure (the casualty may be able to assist you in this respect).

Elevate the limb.

Lay the casualty down.

Apply a sterile dressing (p. 42) and an elevation sling (p. 38) if dealing with forearm or hand wound.

Dial 999 for an ambulance, if needed.

In some less serious instances you may decide that an ambulance is not required. If you decide to transport the casualty to hospital by car, it is sensible for him/her to travel in the back of the vehicle in these circumstances, preferably with a third person to give support and assistance. Remember to take a bucket (or similar) with you in case the casualty feels sick. ***Do not*** transport a casualty in a private vehicle merely because you feel that it will be quicker than waiting for an ambulance.

Problem areas

Bleeding from certain parts of the body can cause problems due to their shape and position. The principles of direct pressure still apply but with variation when it comes to applying a sterile dressing.

Cuts to the scalp and face

These tend to bleed profusely, but rarely endanger the casualty's life. However, superficial scalp and facial wounds can cause distress as the blood gets into the casualty's eyes, nose and mouth. If the casualty is unconscious, you must ensure that the airway is not obstructed by blood – putting the casualty into the recovery position (p. 8) alleviates this problem.

If the bleeding is copious, apply a sterile dressing as best you can, being careful not to obstruct the casualty's vision unless absolutely necessary, and then provide plenty of explanation and reassurance. If the bleeding is not profuse, use a dressing held in place by a light bandage. Always ensure that the casualty can breathe and the bandage is not too tight.

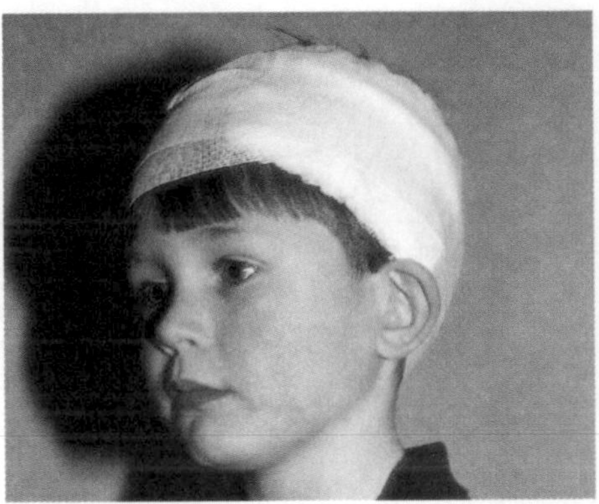

> Always be aware when treating a casualty for scalp and facial wounds that there may be an underlying fracture (p. 56).

Cuts in the palm

Again, this area will bleed profusely and other structures (tendons and nerves) may be damaged. The basic principles of direct pressure and elevation apply, then:

Using a sterile dressing, place the pad on the injured palm and ask the casualty to grip on to this.

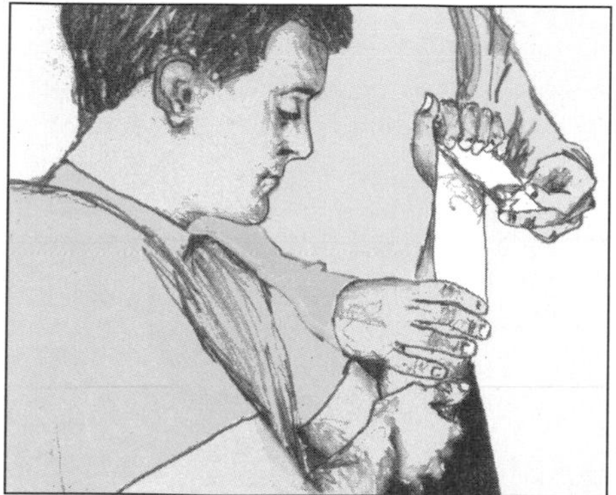

Bandage around the wrist once and then come up and over the fingers so as to apply firm pressure on the wound. Repeat this until the fingers are fully enclosed.

Enclose all the fingers in this way and secure the bandage by tying it over the fingers.

Support the injured hand in an elevation sling (p. 38).

Internal bleeding

Internal bleeding may be completely hidden, in which case the casualty will appear to be shocked without any obvious cause. Such bleeding can occur as a result of an accident or spontaneously and without any warning.

You may notice • Cold, clammy and pale skin.

- Rapid, weakening pulse.
- Discomfort or pain.
- Thirst.
- 'Air hunger' (the casualty yawns frequently).
- Restlessness and irritability.
- Confusion.
- Drowsiness, even lapsing into unconsciousness.

Treatment

Lay the casualty down and, provided there are no lower rib fractures, raise the legs.

Protect the casualty from the cold. Try to place a blanket (or similar) underneath as well as on top.

Loosen any tight clothing at the neck, chest and waist.

Dial 999 for an ambulance.

If the casualty becomes unconscious, perform the ABC of Resuscitation (p. 6).

Bleeding via orifices

On occasions internal bleeding will exhibit itself via an orifice. Such blood loss alerts you to problems that may not otherwise be seen (p. 49).

Cuts in the mouth

Mouth injuries can be serious. While not life-threatening, they can cause considerable discomfort and have long-lasting effects. Very often the injuries sustained are caused by the casualty's teeth.

Ask the casualty to sit down and to lean forward to allow the blood to drain.

Place a piece of gauze over the wound and ask the casualty to squeeze it from the outside and inside with a pincer movement of his/her finger and thumb.

This should be done for 5-10 minutes.

If the bleeding persists, repeat.

> Ask the casualty **not to** swallow any blood as this is likely to cause sickness.

If the wound is minor and does not require medical attention, advise the casualty to avoid hard, chewy foods and hot drinks for 12 hours.

Seek medical aid if the wound is large or if bleeding has not stopped after 20-30 minutes.

Bleeding from the ear

If a casualty has bleeding from the ear, medical advice will need to be sought. If the bleeding is part of a thin, watery loss then you should suspect a head injury (pp. 49 and 110).

Do not plug the ear.

Sit the casualty with the head inclined to the injured side.

Cover the ear with a lightly secured sterile dressing (p. 42).

Arrange for the casualty to go to hospital.

Bleeding from the nose

This is very common following, or during, a cold or as a result of a blow to the nose. If the bleeding is part of a thin, watery loss you should suspect a head injury (pp. 49 and 110). (See also p. 121.)

Do not plug the nose.

Sit the casualty down with the head tipped well forward.

Ask the casualty to pinch the soft part of the nose (just below the upper bony part) and to breathe through the mouth.

Pressure should be applied for at least 10 minutes. If bleeding continues, reapply pressure.

If available, an ice pad can be applied to

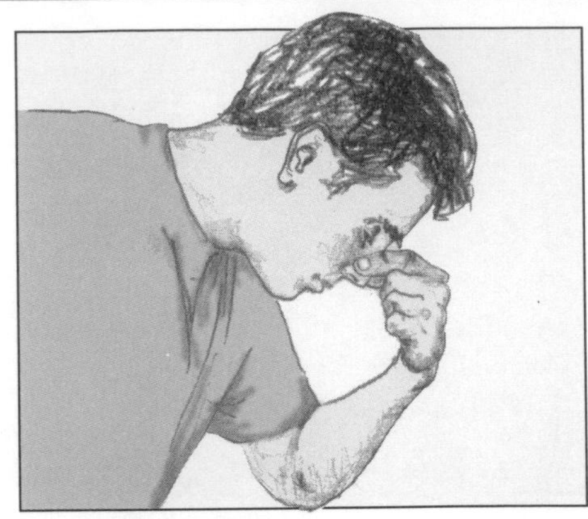

the outside of the nose **in addition** to the above.

1. Seek medical aid if bleeding continues for 20-30 minutes.
2. When bleeding stops, advise the casualty **not to blow nose** for 4-6 hours.

Bleeding from the vagina

A woman suffering unusual or heavy bleeding from her vagina will feel embarrassed and may not seek first aid for some considerable time. Bleeding, when not associated with a normal period, may be due to miscarriage (pp. 49 and 120) or other gynaecological problems.

Treatment

At all times respect the woman's feelings and arrange, if possible, for privacy.

Provide a sanitary pad or a folded hand towel (or similar).

Make the woman comfortable, sit her up with her knees propped up on a couple of blankets (or similar).

If the bleeding is severe, dial 999 for an ambulance.

SEXUAL ASSAULT

- If the woman has been sexually assaulted, you must be most careful to preserve any evidence (p. 128).

Wherever possible, a female should render first aid to a woman with vaginal bleeding. If this is not possible, the male first aider should try to arrange for a female chaperone.

Gunshot Wounds

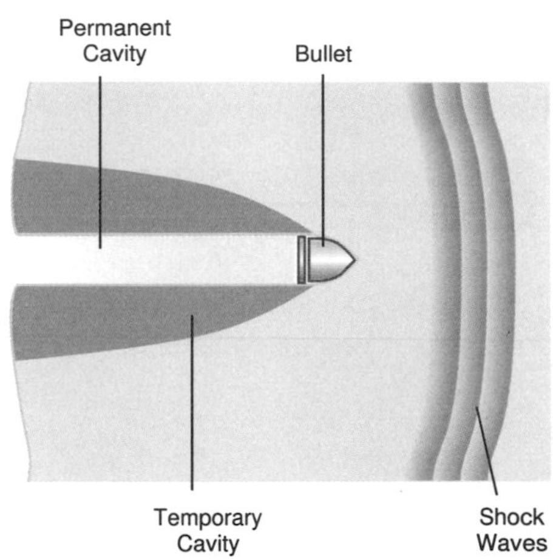

Gunshot wounds are relatively few and far between in the United Kingdom. As with other types of wound, there will be bleeding but due to the nature of gunshot wounds, underlying fractures and internal injuries must always be expected.

Depending on the type of weapon involved, the wounds can vary considerably. High-velocity weapons may cause catastrophic internal damage while leaving only a small entrance wound. Low-velocity weapons cause less severe internal injuries. Airguns may inflict nasty injuries, particularly if the eye is involved, but otherwise generally cause only minor flesh wounds.

TREATMENT

Approach the casualty only if you are sure that it is safe to do so.

If the casualty is unconscious check the ABC of Resuscitation (p. 6) and act accordingly.

Stop any life-threatening bleeding by applying direct pressure on the wound (p. 48).

If an underlying fracture is suspected, immobilise the part (p. 56).

Protect the casualty from the cold.

Do not probe the wounds for the pellet/bullet.

Remember to check for exit wounds. They can be more serious than the entry wound.

Dial 999 for ambulance and police.

Blisters

Blisters are thin 'bubbles' that form on the skin. They occur when the skin is damaged by friction, such as when wearing new shoes or as a consequence of a burn/scald (p. 67).

Under the 'bubble' there is fluid called serum. During the healing process a new skin layer forms. The serum is absorbed before the dead skin peels off.

Treatment

Do not burst the blister.

Cover the blister with a plaster or small dressing (p. 44). Ensure that the pad extends well beyond the edges of the blister.

If a blister has burst

- Clean the area (p. 44).
- **Do not** attempt to peel or cut away the loose skin.
- Cover the area with a plaster or small dressing.

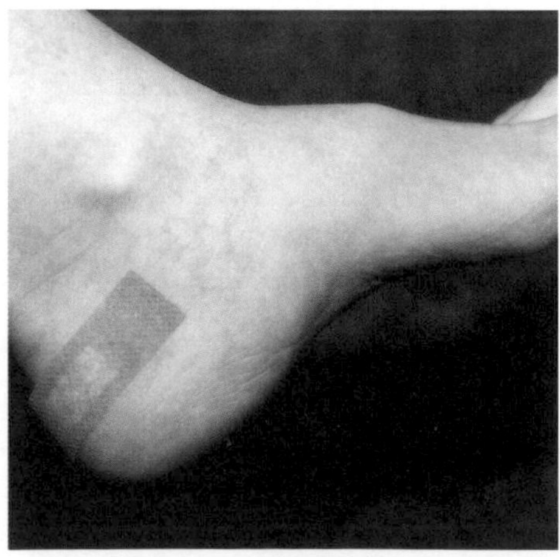

Bone Injuries

There are, broadly speaking, two types of bone injury that concern the first aider. One is a fracture, or break in a bone. The other is a dislocation, where the bone at a joint becomes displaced from its normal position. The skeleton is an internal framework which supports the body's organs, muscles and tissues. When a bone injury occurs, damage is not limited to the bone itself: the surrounding tissues and their functions are also affected. Commonly, the ability to move a limb is impaired, but in some cases vital structures that lie alongside the bone can be damaged.

Fractures

A fracture is a break or crack in a bone. In adult life considerable force is required to cause a fracture. Children's bones are more flexible and supple and, on occasion, 'split' or crack, causing a greenstick fracture. In the elderly, the bones become less resilient and prone to breaking more easily, particularly the neck of the femur in the hip.

Fractures can be further complicated by the presence of a wound over the site of the break; this is called an open fracture. A break without a surface wound is called a closed fracture.

Fractures can be caused either by direct force or indirect force. Direct force is a blow that affects the bone under its impact point, causing a fracture. In indirect force, the power of an impact is transmitted from the point of contact to cause a fracture at a distant point. This type of fracture can be caused by a twisting action, say at the ankle, that breaks a bone in the leg, or by jumping/falling, such as when a person lands on the outstretched hand with the arm braced, and fractures the collar bone.

General principles

Whatever the type of fracture, your priorities are the same. It may be that due to the overall nature of the casualty's injuries you do not treat them, but rather concentrate on life-saving first aid.

PRIORITIES

- ABC of Resuscitation.
- Control of bleeding.
- Immobilisation of the fracture.

You will notice • Discomfort around the fracture site.

- A history of a recent fall, blow, etc.

You may notice • Swelling and bruising developing.

- Pain.
- Shortening of an affected limb.
- Unusual shape.
- A grating sound if the bone ends move.
- Difficulty in movement.

1. With fractures of the small bones of the wrist and ankle there may be normal movement associated with severe discomfort but little visible sign of injury.
2. With fractures of bones that cover and protect the body's organs (skull, ribs and pelvis), always suspect underlying injury to an organ.

Dislocations

Following a strong wrenching force or a violent contraction of the muscles, it is possible for a bone to become displaced at a joint. Dislocations most commonly occur at the shoulder, finger, thumb and jaw. It is often difficult to distinguish a fracture from a dislocation.

You will notice • Swelling.

• Discomfort.

• History of recent fall, blow, etc.

You may notice • Pain.

• Unusual shape to a joint area.

• Bruising developing.

Open Fractures

This is where there is a wound over the site of the fracture. The bone may or may not be protruding.

Cover the wound and immobilise as for a closed fracture.

Bone Protruding

- Build up pads of non-fluffy material around the protruding bone.
- Cover the area with a sterile dressing.
- ***Do not* try to push the bone back into the wound.**
- Check the circulation on a toe/finger below the fracture (p. 40).
- Treat as for a closed fracture.

If the bone is not protruding, gently cover the wound with a sterile dressing.

Once the wound is covered treat as for a closed fracture.

Treatment Summary

Whatever the bone injury, the treatment is the same. If you have any doubt about an injury that may have damaged a bone, **always** treat it as a fracture. The general principles are to:

Immobilise the affected part.

Provide support to the area.

Summon medical help.

Skull Fractures

If you suspect a skull fracture, always treat the casualty as a suspected head injury (p. 110).

Treatment

If the casualty is unconscious, follow the ABC of Resuscitation (p. 6) and treat appropriately.

If the casualty is conscious, lay him/her down with the head and shoulders raised and supported.

Dial 999 for an ambulance.

Suspect skull fractures

WHEN YOU NOTICE:

- A wound or bruise on the head or around the eyes.
- A soft area on the scalp.
- A depression on the scalp.
- A thin, watery, bloodstained discharge from the ear or nose.
- An unusual shape to part of the head.

Facial Injuries

The facial bones are vulnerable to fracture following direct force. The nose, cheekbones and jaw are the most commonly affected. Additionally, teeth may have been dislodged or loosened and the soft tissues of the mouth and upper airway can become swollen.

Major facial injuries

Major injuries to the face can cause serious problems. The soft tissues can rapidly become very swollen and this, combined with bleeding and distorted facial anatomy, may lead to the casualty's airway becoming blocked. Major facial injuries may have associated brain and spinal injuries (p. 132). Casualties with major facial injuries may be unconscious.

Treatment

Clear the casualty's airway (p. 7).

Turn the casualty to the recovery position (p. 8).

Dial 999 for an ambulance.

Less serious facial injuries

These types of injuries cause extreme discomfort and **always** require sending the casualty to hospital.

Treatment

Treat any nose bleed (p. 52).

Arrange for the casualty to be taken to hospital.

1. A cold compress placed over the fracture site may relieve the discomfort.
2. A pad held in place by the casualty may support the injured parts and relieve some of the discomfort.

Jaw Injuries

Facial injuries commonly entail injury to the jaw. The jaw is a hinged bone that can be fractured or may dislocate, usually as a result of a direct blow. However, some people can be unfortunate enough to experience a spontaneous dislocation, often while yawning.

Injury to the jaw, in association with widespread facial injuries, may cause obstruction of the casualty's airway due to swelling.

You will notice • Reluctance to open the mouth or inability to close it.

• Pain.

You may notice • Distorted face.

• Distorted teeth.

• Dribbling.

• Swelling and pain.

- Discomfort while swallowing.
- A wound in the mouth or around the lower face (jaw).
- Difficulty in speaking.

TREATMENT

Sit the casualty down with the head well forward so as to allow blood and other secretions to drain.

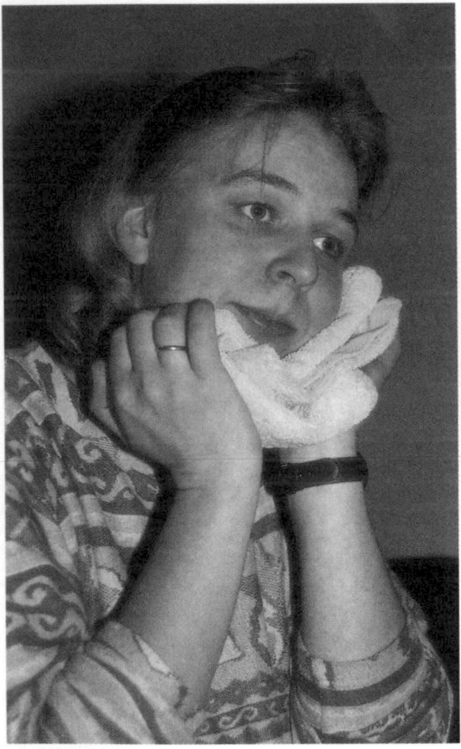

Ask the casualty to support the jaw by holding a soft pad around it.

Dial 999 for an ambulance.

If vomiting occurs, help the casualty to support the jaw and to continue leaning forward. Gently clean out the casualty's mouth as best you can; ***do not*** offer anything to drink.

JAW INJURY AND OTHER FACIAL INJURIES

- Lie the casualty down, supported on the side so as to keep the airway clear.
- Place padding under the jaw and other injuries so as to lessen any discomfort.

Fractured Ribs

The ribs form a protective cage for the lungs, heart and major blood vessels. If the ribs have been broken, it may be that the lungs have been punctured. If a wound is present you should suspect air entering the chest cavity (pneumothorax).

TREATMENT

Care for the conscious casualty in a position he/she finds comfortable.

Any open wounds over the chest area should be promptly covered to make an airtight seal (p. 124).

If the casualty becomes unconscious, place him/her in the recovery position with the injured side resting against the ground.

Fractured Pelvis

Always suspect a fractured pelvis if the casualty has been crushed across the upper legs/lower abdomen or when the car casualty has a fractured thigh as a result of a road accident.

You may notice • Inability to walk/stand – even if the legs appear uninjured.

- Pain in hips, groin, back or abdomen.
- Urge, but inability, to pass urine.
- Shock.

TREATMENT

Help the casualty to lie on his/her back.

Support the legs in the most comfortable position.

Treat the casualty for shock (p. 129).

Dial 999 for an ambulance.

INTERNAL BLEEDING

If a casualty has a fractured pelvis, always suspect internal injuries with associated internal bleeding.

Shoulder Injuries

Shoulder injuries may be due to a fracture of the head of the humerus (upper arm bone), a dislocated shoulder or a fractured scapula (shoulder-blade).

TREATMENT

Support the injured arm in a broad arm sling (p. 37).

Arrange for the casualty to go to hospital.

Collar bone Injuries

Following a fall on to an outstretched arm or by direct force, the collar bone may fracture.

You may notice • The casualty inclines the head on to the injured side.

TREATMENT

Support the arm on the injured side in an elevation sling (p. 38).

Send the casualty to hospital.

Arm Injuries

Very often the casualty will support the injured arm across the body. Use a sling to help support the arm.

WHICH SLING TO USE

Broad arm sling (p. 37)	Dislocated shoulder Fractured upper arm Fractured forearm Fractured wrist
Elevation sling (p. 38)	Fractures to the hand Dislocations of the finger/thumb Fractured collar bone

Arrange for the casualty to go to hospital.

Fractured Elbow

A fracture around the site of the elbow can be extremely painful. It is a relatively common injury; children particularly are prone to fracturing the humerus (upper arm bone) just above the elbow.

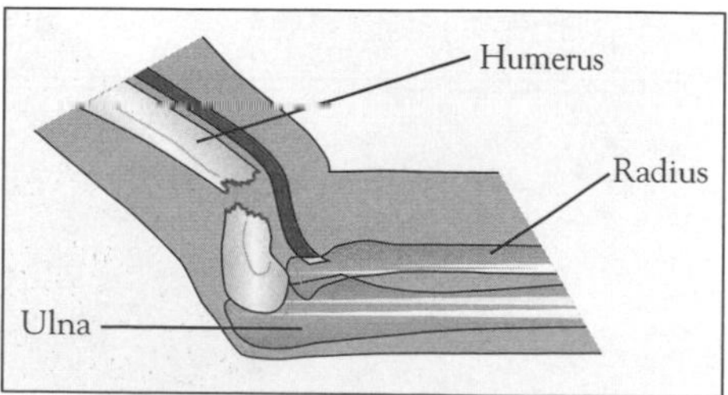

This type of fracture is unstable and can cause damage to the surrounding blood vessels and nerves. For this reason, it is very important to check the pulse at the casualty's wrist frequently.

Another common fracture that occurs around the elbow is to the head of the radius following a fall on to the hand.

In the case of a fractured elbow, you will notice the same signs and symptoms as with other fractures, with one possible addition.

You may notice • The elbow is very stiff if the head of the radius has been fractured.

TREATMENT

If the casualty is supporting the arm across the chest, apply a broad arm sling.

If the arm is not supported across the chest, immobilise the arm by splinting it to the body in the position that was adopted by the casualty.

Do this by preparing two broad-fold triangular bandages (p. 39) with padding.

Pad under the arm so as to cushion the injury, using anything soft.

Place one broad-fold bandage above the elbow around the body and tie it on the far side of the body from the injury.

Place the other broad-fold bandage below the elbow around the body and tie it on the far side of the body from the injury.

Dial 999 for an ambulance.

Check the pulse at the wrist on the affected side every 10 minutes.

> Where a broad arm sling is used and the injury is painful or you expect a bumpy journey, provide additional support.
>
> 1. Put a folded towel (or similar) between the casualty's arm and body.
> 2. Place a broad-fold triangular bandage (p. 39) around the casualty and the affected arm, over the sling, and tie off on the far side of the body from the injury.

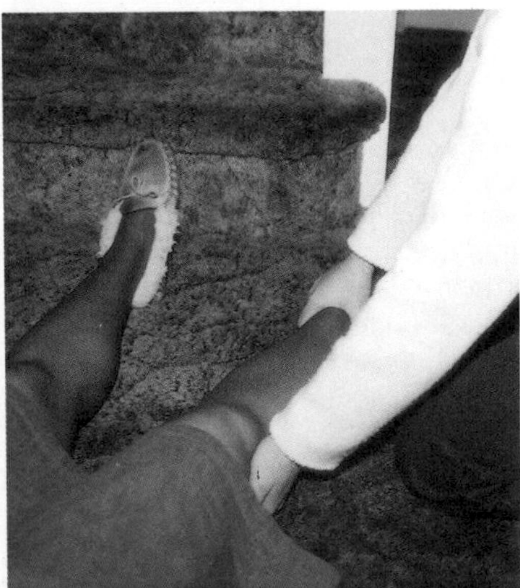

Fractured Leg

In addition to the general symptoms you may notice when a fracture has occurred, leg fractures can show additional signs:

You may notice • Shortening of the leg.

• Obvious deformity of the leg.

TREATMENT

Tell the casualty not to move the leg.

Support the leg, if you can, in the position that it was found. Do this by holding the leg: one hand well above the fracture site and one below.

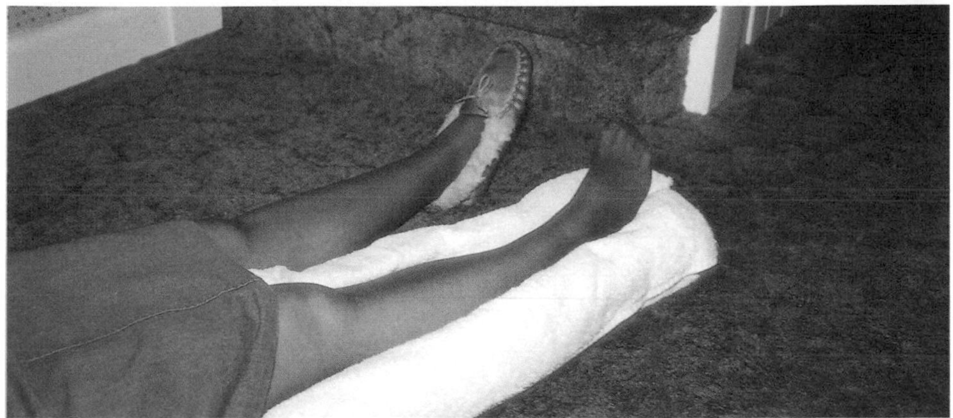

If available, use rolled-up towels (or similar) to prevent the leg from moving. Place the towels both on the inside as well as the outside of the injured leg, ensuring that the knee and ankles are well supported.

Dial 999 for an ambulance.

If you suspect that help is going to be delayed in arriving, or you are unable to support the injured leg by the method described above, do the following:

Move the **uninjured leg** to lie alongside the injured leg.

Continue to provide support to the injured leg throughout.

Place soft padding between the casualty's legs, paying particular attention to the knees and ankles.

Tie the casualty's ankles together using a narrow-fold triangular bandage (p. 39):

Pass one end of the bandage under the casualty's ankles, cross the two ends over (do not tie a knot) on top of the ankles, pass each end around the foot and tie off the bandage on the bottom of the foot.

Use a broad-fold triangular bandage to go around the casualty's knees and tie off on the uninjured side.

Fractured Hip

This is a common injury in the elderly, particularly women, following a fall. The neck of the femur fractures, causing a shortening of the limb associated with the foot of the affected leg being turned outward.

Treat as for a fractured leg.

Knee Injuries

The knee is a large, hinged joint in the middle of the leg that is supported by very strong muscles and ligaments. At the front of the knee is the kneecap which serves to protect the joint behind.

Damage and injury can occur due to direct force, twisting (particularly if sudden and violent) and strains.

You may notice • Pain in and around the knee.

• The kneecap may be displaced or feel indented across its surface.

• Swelling of the knee.

• Severe and deep-seated pain on trying to straighten the knee.

• The knee is 'locked', often bent.

Do not try to force the knee straight.

Do not allow the casualty to walk; **in an emergency** he/she can hop on the good leg with support.

Treatment

Lay the casualty down.

Support the injured knee in the most comfortable position for the casualty.

Dial 999 for an ambulance.

> If the casualty's knee is 'locked' or is more comfortable kept bent, place rolled up blankets, clothes, etc. under the knee to provide support.

Fractured Feet

Fractures of the small bones of the feet are often caused by crush injuries, although occasionally the heel bone can be fractured by over-enthusiastic stamping of the foot on to the ground heel first, jumping from a height, etc.

Treatment

Send the casualty to hospital.

If possible, elevate the foot (this should continue during the journey to hospital).

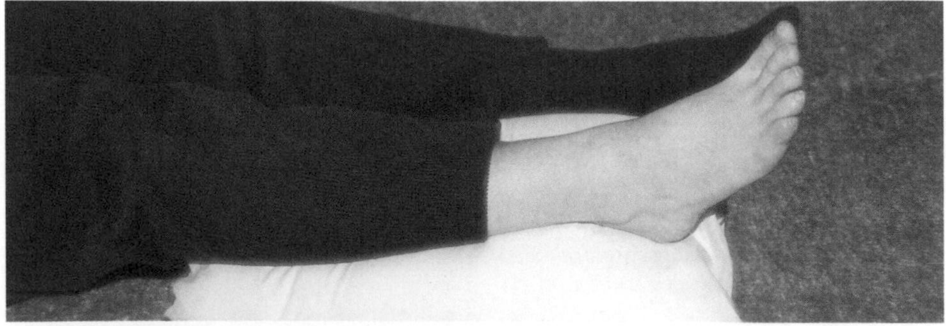

Breathing Problems

Breathing problems may be caused by illness such as asthma (p. 34), from infection, abdominal pain, stress (hyperventilation) or as a result of injury. Whatever the cause, problems occur when someone cannot breathe properly and their body's oxygen level becomes lowered.

Hypoxia

If the problem is severe, the casualty will become extremely unwell due to the effects of a severely lowered oxygen level (hypoxia).

You will notice • Rapid, very distressed breathing.

- Confusion.
- Irritability and aggression.
- Blueness of the skin.

If the hypoxia is not treated promptly the casualty will become unconscious and, in extreme cases, stop breathing.

Suffocation

When air is prevented from entering the lungs the casualty is said to have suffocated. This may be due to a gas- or fume- filled atmosphere, or the smothering of the casualty's mouth and nose.

If the cause of the suffocation is due to a gas- or fume-filled atmosphere, remove the casualty into the fresh air (**only if it is safe for you to do so**).

Treatment

Clear the casualty's face, chest and abdomen of any debris.

If the casualty is unconscious, perform the ABC of Resuscitation (p. 6) and treat as appropriate.

All victims of suffocation, even if conscious following rescue, must go to hospital as a matter of urgency. Dial 999 for an ambulance.

Inhaling Fumes

Depending on the source of the fumes, the effect on the casualty may be fatal. Any first aider who attends the scene may also be in very grave danger.

Safety

- Do not put yourself at risk if there is any possibility that you will be overcome by the fumes.

Treatment

Dial 999 **first,** ask for the fire brigade as well as the ambulance service.

If safe to do so, evacuate the casualty into fresh air.

If the casualty is unconscious, check the ABC of Resuscitation and treat as appropriate (p. 6).

Hanging and Strangling

Hanging and strangling constrict the casualty's neck so that air cannot get into the lungs.

TREATMENT

Remove any constriction from around the casualty's neck.

If the casualty is unconscious, check the ABC of Resuscitation and treat as appropriate (p. 6).

Dial 999 for an ambulance, even if recovery seems to be complete.

THE HANGING CASUALTY

- Try to support the casualty's body so as to relieve the pressure on the neck until he/she can be cut down.
- The police will require any nooses, etc.; keep them safe.

Hyperventilation

Uncontrollable overbreathing (hyperventilation) is often associated with an acute anxiety attack or panic attack.

You will notice • Rapid, deep breathing.

You may notice • Feeling of dizziness or faintness.

• Complaint of tingling in the hands.

TREATMENT

Remain calm, show patience and great kindness to the casualty.

Remove the casualty to a quiet area away from any cause of the panicking.

Encourage the casualty deliberately to slow the rate of breathing to a more normal pattern.

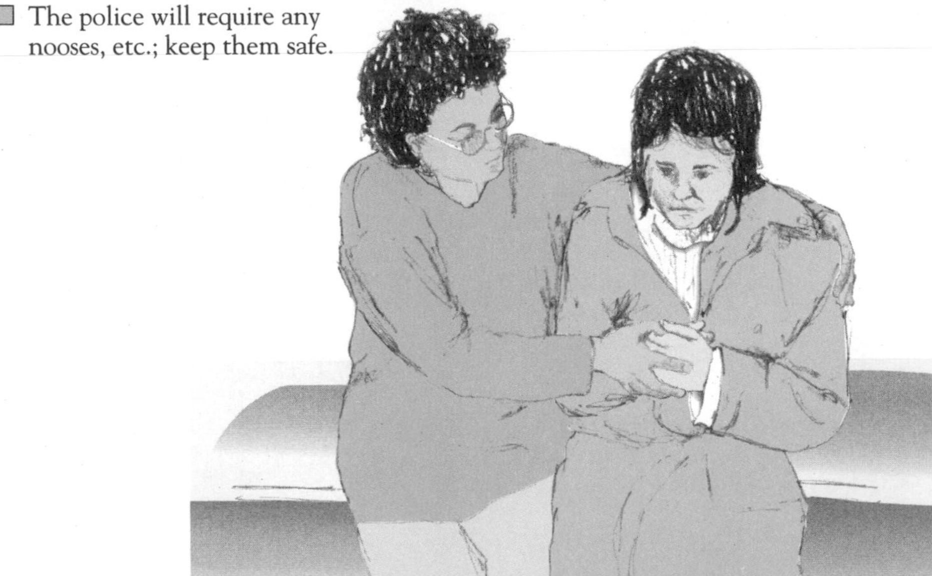

> If the casualty is unable to gain control of breathing after 5 minutes, or is unable to attempt to do so, get him/her to breathe in and out of a **paper bag** until the breathing becomes normal.

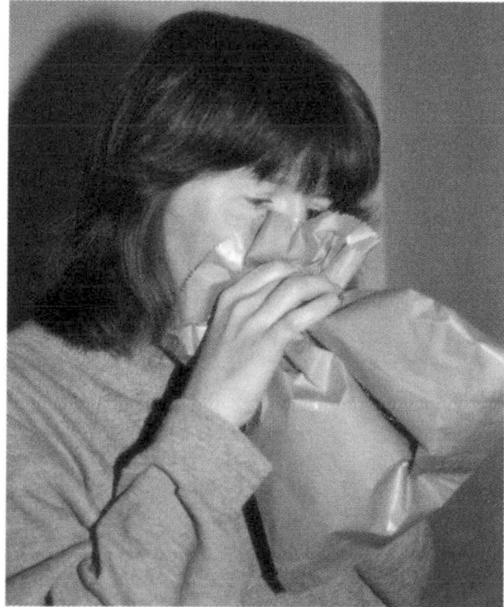

If the casualty remains in a state of hyperventilation after 20-30 minutes – summon medical aid.

Hiccups

Also known as hiccoughs; these are caused by the diaphragm contracting suddenly and repeatedly. Each contraction causes a short expulsion of air that makes the familiar hiccup noise as it encounters the trachea that is normally blocked off.

Attacks are usually of a few minutes duration but it is possible that they can be more prolonged (even days and in a very few instances weeks). Then they are not only tiring, but painful.

Treatment

Advise the casualty to take a very deep breath and to hold it for as long as possible OR

Use a paper bag; the casualty should be advised to rebreathe his/her own expired air by holding the bag over the nose and mouth. Continue for 3-5 minutes OR

Help the casualty to take a drink from the wrong side of a glass.

If the hiccups persist after 2-3 hours, seek medical advice.

Sudden Breathing Problems

On occasions, otherwise fit and healthy individuals can suddenly suffer difficulties with breathing. This may be due to a number of reasons, including asthma (p. 34) or a collapsed lung.

You will notice • Rapid breathing (may be deep or shallow).

• Distress.

You may notice • Rapid pulse.

• Blueish skin.

Treatment

If the casualty is unconscious, check the ABC of Resuscitation and treat as appropriate (p. 6).

If the casualty is conscious, move into a comfortable sitting position.

Loosen tight clothing at the neck, chest and waist.

Dial 999 for an ambulance.

Bruises

A bruise is a result of bleeding occurring under the skin. It can be very extensive, for instance, when associated with a major fracture; or it can be very minor, as with everyday knocks and bumps.

If the bruising is severe and extensive, always suspect an underlying fracture or internal injuries.

You will notice • A discoloured area (mottled blue/mauve in the early stages).

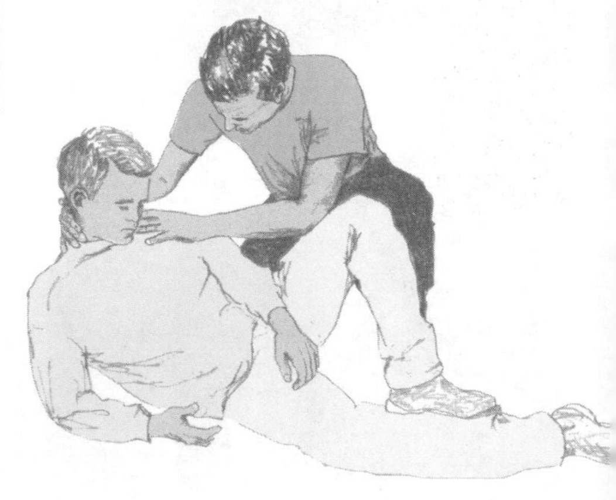

TREATMENT

If you suspect any underlying injury, treat as appropriate.

For minor bruising apply a cold compress for 15 minutes.

Advise the casualty to soak in a warm bath to ease the discomfort.

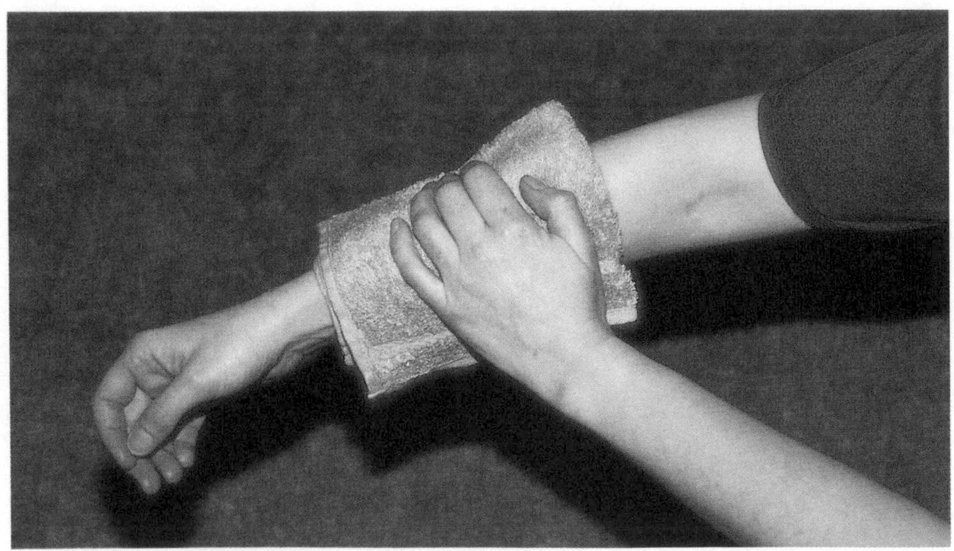

Burns and Scalds

Burns are due to dry heat (including friction) whereas scalds are due to wet heat. It is most important that burns and scalds are treated promptly and correctly so as to limit the effects of the injury and to prevent possible long-term scarring.

Assessing a burn/scald

There are two factors in assessing the severity of burns and scalds: depth and extent of the injury.

Depth of burns/scalds

Superficial

The skin is reddened and may be swollen. This type of burn/scald is painful.

Partial thickness

The skin is blistered and raw. This type of burn/scald is painful. Extensive burns/scalds of this type can be fatal.

Full thickness

The skin is burnt away and the damage extends into the muscle and fat layers. There is a pale, waxy look to the burn with charred areas also possible. Because the nerve endings have been damaged, these types of burns/scalds involve little or no pain.

Extent of burns

To assess the extent of burns, the body is divided into percentage areas. Using the chart, you can assess what level of care your casualty requires.

Very often two or three categories of burn may be found within one wound; always treat as for the most serious type present.

TYPE OF BURN	EXTENT	REFERRAL
Superficial	9% or less	Own doctor
Partial Thickness	1-8%	Own doctor
	9% or more	999
Full Thickness	Any size	999

NB When assessing the size of casualty's burns remember that 1% = the size of the casualty's hand.

WHEN TO SUSPECT BURNS/SCALDS TO THE THROAT AND MOUTH

- ☐ The face has been burned.
- ☐ There is soot around the mouth or around and in the nostrils.
- ☐ The history of the incident suggests that the casualty has been inhaling hot fumes.
- ☐ The casualty's voice starts to become hoarse.

Burns to the mouth and throat

Swelling occurs rapidly following a burn/scald. For this reason, any burn to the mouth or throat must be treated as an emergency. Whenever all of the face has been burnt/scalded, **always** presume the mouth and throat have also been affected.

TREATMENT

Dial 999 immediately.

Loosen tight clothing around the neck, chest and waist.

IF THE CASUALTY BECOMES UNCONSCIOUS

- If the burn/scald is due to chemical contamination, be sure that you are not placing yourself at risk before starting resuscitation.
- Check the ABC of Resuscitation and treat as appropriate (p. 6).

Serious burns/scalds

Dial 999 immediately.

Gently flood the affected areas with copious amounts of water (or other cold, non-flammable liquid, e.g. beer or milk).

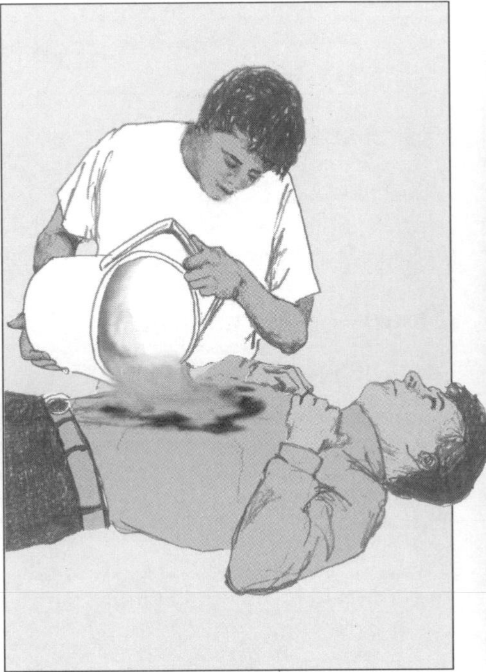

Remove any clothing that is not sticking to the burn/scald.

Cover the affected area as soon as possible and continue to apply water over the covering.

Treat the casualty for shock (p. 129).

COVERING BURNS

This is very important so as to stop the area becoming infected. Use:

- Non-fluffy material (e.g. pillow case or similar).

- Kitchen film (discard the first 2 turns from the roll).
- Hands and feet can be enclosed in a clean plastic bag.

Do not waste time by trying to secure such coverings in place.

Be very careful not to lower the casualty's body temperature to the point where hypothermia sets in. Follow these rules when cooling a casualty.

Wrap the casualty in a blanket (or similar).

Use buckets or jugs of cold water to douse the affected area – even over the covering.

Do not immerse the casualty in a bath full of cold water.

Do not apply lotions, creams, butter, cooking fat, etc. They do not cool the burn and have to be cleaned off in the hospital.

Do not completely enclose burned limbs with kitchen film or other material; as the limb starts to swell it is possible that the circulation to the area beyond the burn may be cut off.

Minor burns and scalds

These are very common and will heal well provided first aid is carried out promptly and efficiently.

Treatment

Hold the affected area under a running cold water tap for at least 10-15 minutes, or until the pain stops.

Remove any jewellery from the affected area before swelling starts.

Do not use any creams, lotions, butter or cooking oil to assist with cooling; they often make matters worse.

Blistered or raw areas: cover with a non-fluffy dressing such as a sterile dressing or plaster (pp. 42 and 44). If the area becomes infected, seek medical advice.

Dos and Don'ts for Minor Burns and Scalds

- ***Do not*** burst any blisters.
- ***Do not*** use adhesive tape to hold a dressing in place.
- ***Do not*** use creams, lotions, butter or cooking oils to 'cool' a burn/scald.
- ***Do*** seek medical help if you are worried for any reason about a burn/scald.

The Electrocuted Casualty

The major concern when dealing with a casualty who has received an electric shock is **safety** – yours and the casualty's!

Ensure that the current is switched off before touching the casualty. Do this either at the wall switch or fuse box.

If this is not possible use a non-conducting object such as a wooden pole to knock the source of electricity from the casualty.

Do not approach any casualty who is in a sub-station or on a railway line until the current has been turned off and you are given permission to do so by a person in authority.

Chemical Burns

Chemicals in common use around the home are not very corrosive but never the less should be treated with respect.
In case of a chemical burn, flood the affected area with water until professional help arrives (wear rubber gloves if you are helping someone else). Beware of fumes and further contamination.

DIAL 999 IN ALL CASES OF ELECTRICAL AND CHEMICAL BURNS

Fire

When someone's clothing is on fire, the action you take will be vital to his/her well-being. Of course, your chief concern will be to put the flames out.

If someone is on fire

- Lay the casualty down with the burning uppermost.
- Douse the flames with any non-flammable liquid, e.g. water, milk, etc

OR

- Wrap the casualty up tightly in a blanket, coat, rug, etc. (**not nylon, polyester or other manmade fabrics**).
- Lay the wrapped casualty on the ground.

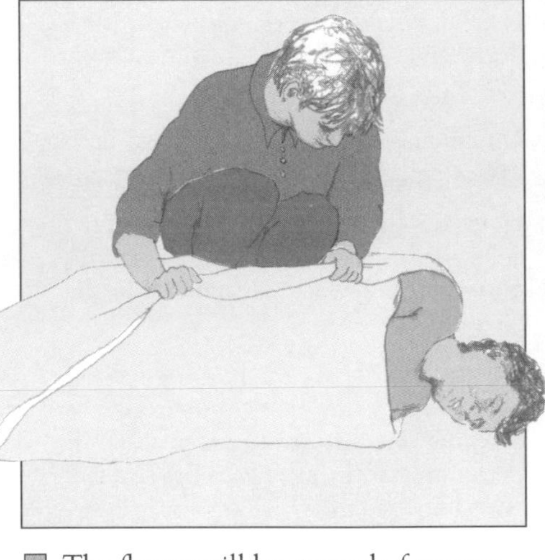

- The flames will be starved of oxygen and will go out.

Do not allow the casualty to rush around.

Do not beat at the flames with a coat, etc.

Do not roll the casualty along the ground.

If you do any of the above, the flames will 'jump around' – they will spread, causing further burns.

Once the flames are out – treat the casualty for burns (p. 68).

Casualty Examination

On many occasions it is not necessary to make a full examination of a casualty who has sustained an injury that is localised both in cause and effect, e.g. cutting a finger with the kitchen knife, catching someone's arm with an accidental blow, etc. However, there are circumstances when things are not so clear cut and a full casualty examination has to be performed.

When to perform a casualty examination

- When the casualty is unconscious or semi-conscious.
- Following a heavy fall or when thrown.
- When the casualty is uncertain as to what has happened.
- If you suspect injuries that the casualty may not be aware of.

IF IN DOUBT – EXAMINE

Guidelines for making an examination

A good casualty examination is much more than a quick body search. It needs to be conducted with sensitivity, even if the casualty is unconscious. At all times, the first aider must attempt to preserve the casualty's dignity (as well as body warmth). Once you have made sure the casualty is breathing, you need to ascertain whether there is any serious bleeding. Only when you are sure that life is not endangered, do you proceed to perform a more detailed examination, looking for fractures, cuts and grazes, etc. and trying to determine the cause.

What you may expect to find

Fall from a low wall	Possible fracture (including skull) Cuts and grazes Possible unconsciousness/ head injury Shock
Fall from a height	Possible multiple fractures Internal bleeding Head injury/unconsciousness Spinal injury Shock
Casualty in the front of a car	Fractures of legs and arms Pelvic fractures Cuts and grazes Spinal injury Head injury/unconsciousness Rib and chest injuries (particularly with drivers) Shock
Casualty in the back of a car	Fractures of legs and arms Facial injuries Spinal injuries Head injury/unconsciousness Cuts and grazes Shock

NB Expect severe injuries if a casualty is not wearing a seat belt.

FREQUENTLY ASSOCIATED COMPLICATIONS

Head injury	Spinal injury
Head injury	Brain injury
Chest Injury	Spinal injury
Head and chest injuries	Spinal injury
Fractures of both thigh bones	Pelvic fracture
Pelvic fracture	Internal injuries
Rib/chest injuries	Internal injuries
Shock (with no apparent injury)	Internal bleeding
Central chest pain for more than 5 minutes	Heart attack
Watery bloodstained fluid from ear and nose	Skull fracture

This list is not exhaustive and each casualty is unique; however, certain types of accidents do commonly present the first aider with certain types of injuries.

The presence of certain types of injuries should also serve to alert the first aider to the possibility of a casualty having further injuries.

Diagnosis

It must be emphasised that any diagnosis made by a first aider will always be very basic. **The Golden Rule in first aid is: 'If you suspect it – treat for it.'** On this basis it is, therefore, acceptable that, as a first aid measure, any victim of trauma should always be treated as if for a spinal injury (p. 132). Indeed, most trauma specialists would advocate this approach.

How to make a casualty examination

Priorities

Safety.

Establish Consciousness Level.

ABC of Resuscitation.

Body Check for Bleeding.

Detailed Body Check.

Once it is safe to approach the casualty, do so.

Try to rouse, but do not move, the casualty. Speak loudly to him/her and gently shake the shoulders.

Perform ABC of Resuscitation (p. 6).

RESUSCITATION

- The ABC of Resuscitation (p. 6) takes priority over everything else.
- Remember to control serious bleeding early in your attempts to resuscitate.
- Ask someone else to apply direct pressure and elevate the injured part.

Examining the casualty

Starting at the head and taking care not to move the head and neck, quickly run your hands over the casualty to check for bleeding.

Do this by being systematic:
Head.
Chest.
Abdomen.
Legs.
Arms.

Remember to search underneath the casualty as best you can, and frequently check your hands for blood.

Do not allow yourself to be diverted by the finding of fractures or less serious bleeding – they can wait.

Treat any serious bleeding (p. 48).

You can now begin your more detailed examination. Without moving the casualty's head and neck, gently feel over the scalp for any unusual bumps or depressions indicating a skull fracture. Look into the casualty's eyes to see if the pupils are equal in size and respond to light. Check the ears and nose for signs of any bleeding. Gently, and without moving the head and neck, feel along the line of the bones of the spine from the base of the skull to as far down the casualty's upper back as you can manage. Check for a stoma (opening) in the neck; look under any scarf/cravat. Loosen any tight clothing at the neck and check for an SOS/Medic-alert talisman.

Now start to check the rest of the body. Run your hands firmly down the front of the casualty's chest and repeat this down the side of the chest, starting at the armpits. You may notice a 'spongy feel' to part of the chest wall or an unusual shape, both of which indicate the presence of a fracture. If there is a chest wound, always suspect that air is getting into the chest. Reassess the breathing. Is the casualty gasping or taking irregular breaths? If breathing appears to be absent, recheck the ABC of Resuscitation (p. 6).

Firmly run your hands over the casualty's abdomen. Is it unusually firm (indicating possible internal bleeding)? Is there a wound? Does the casualty wince or cry out, indicating pain?

Now feel the pelvis bones. Place a hand on each side of the pelvis and carefully rock the pelvis. If the casualty complains of pain or discomfort or if you detect any 'give' in the normally rigid pelvis, suspect a fracture. Check for incontinence.

As best you can, move your hand into the small of the casualty's back. Be careful not to rock or otherwise move the casualty. Gently feel up and down the spine for unusual swelling and observe for any signs of tenderness.

Now move to the lower limbs, examining each one separately, starting at the top. As best you can, encompass the limb, using your hands, and slide them down the leg, feeling for wounds, swelling or deformity. Remember to include the ankle and knee. If there is nothing obviously wrong, ask the casualty to raise one leg and move knees, ankles and toes.

Finally, examine the arms in much the same way as the legs. Examine them one at a time and encompass the casualty's arm with your hands. Slide your hands down the casualty's arm, feeling for wounds, swelling or deformity. Once you are sure that there is nothing obviously wrong, ask the casualty to move an arm and to bend and straighten shoulder, elbow, wrist and fingers.

WHAT TO LOOK FOR

ABC of Resuscitation	See page 6
Serious Bleeding	Rapid pulse Pale, cold and clammy skin Lots of blood
Spinal Injury	The history of the accident suggests the spine may have been injured Significant head and/or chest injuries Swelling or deformity around the spine which may be associated with pain Altered sensation, i.e. loss of feeling, the limbs feel heavy or numb, the presence of tingling or burning sensations
Bone Injuries	Deformity Swelling and pain Wounds over possible fracture
Breathing Problems	Abnormally fast or slow breathing Unequal movement from part of the chest wall Pain associated with breathing
Abdominal Problems	Tender abdomen Rigid/unusually hard abdomen Pain/discomfort
Miscellaneous	Casualty's colour Level of consciousness

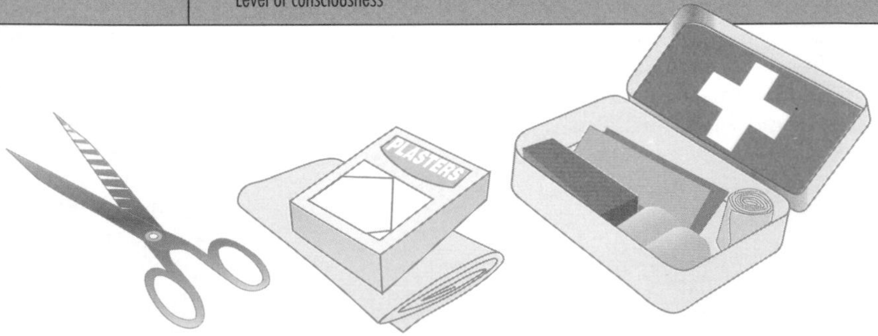

Childbirth

Childbirth is usually a prolonged process that gives time for help to arrive. Very rarely, a woman will have a rapid labour and deliver a baby before professional help is at hand. Often, a sense of panic sets in when a woman starts to experience her labour pains. If the waters should break, then the delivery is expected to be imminent and panic increases. Quite simply, it is worth remembering that women have been giving birth for thousands of years and for much of that time there was no midwifery or medical care.

The Rapid Birth

On the very few occasions when this does occur, be reassured that experienced advice is always close at hand. The woman herself will almost certainly have had previous children and possesses a natural instinct as to when to push and bear down. It is unusual for the rapid birth to be complicated by a baby lying in an abnormal position.

Rely on the woman to decide when the birth is imminent – she will be right!

Do not try to delay the birth.

Do not try to keep the baby inside the mother's birth canal.

Ask others to phone for help.

If time permits, try to obtain some privacy for the woman – she may be able to walk to a secluded area or temporary screens may be available.

Help the woman to remove her underwear, i.e. tights, panties, etc.

Help the woman to adopt a comfortable position. Whether she is lying on her back or squatting, try to place clean sheets or towels under her.

Ask others to get clean towels or similar to wrap the baby in.

Remind yourself not to panic.

If there is time, wash your hands.

If the woman is leaking faeces from her back passage, you must clean the area with suitable materials. **Always** wipe from the front towards the back; this prevents contaminating the woman's vagina (front passage) and the baby.

As the perineum (area between the woman's legs) starts to bulge, be ready to support the baby's head as it is born.

Do not try to pull or wiggle the head free; simply provide support so that it is delivered into your hands.

As soon as the head is delivered check to see that the mouth and nose are clear of the membrane that surrounds the baby in the womb. If necessary, use your fingers to pull the membrane away; it will tear easily.

As soon as the neck is visible, look to see if the umbilical cord is wrapped around the baby's neck. If so, lift it over the baby's head.

The baby's head will start to turn with its body so that it faces sideways. This is quite normal and you should continue to provide support to the head.

One shoulder will be born before the other. Once this has occurred, lift the baby up towards the mother's abdomen. This will deliver the other shoulder and allow the rest of the baby to be born very quickly.

Do not pull the baby's head.

Do not manipulate/wiggle the baby's head.

Do not pull at the baby's shoulders.

The baby will be very wet and slippery and will remain attached to the mother through the umbilical cord. ***Do not*** **attempt to cut the cord.**

Lay the baby on the mother's abdomen and gently clean around its mouth and nose with clean material, e.g. gauze, handkerchief.

The baby should start to take its first breaths and to cry. You do not need to smack the baby to stimulate it.

If the baby does not start to breathe then carry out the ABC of Resuscitation for babies (p. 15).

Wrap the baby in blankets or towels. Remember to enclose its head so that just the face remains clear.

GIVE THE BABY TO THE MOTHER

- The cord is long enough for the baby to be cuddled by the mother.
- Many mothers wish to put their baby to the breast as soon as possible after birth.
- Keep the baby on its side with its head slightly lower than the rest of its body so as to allow any fluids and mucus to drain.

Delivering the placenta

This will occur naturally within about 30 minutes. It is usually associated with a small amount of bleeding.

THE CORD

- The cord should be left uncut until professional help arrives.
- It may palpate for a short while.

Do not attempt to tug the placenta free by pulling on the cord.

Place the delivered placenta into a plastic bag (or similar); it will need to be inspected by the midwife or doctor so as to ensure that no fragments of it have been retained inside the mother.

HEAVY BLEEDING AFTER THE DELIVERY

- This is rare.
- Massage the woman's lower abdomen over the womb so as to encourage contraction of the uterus.
- Continue massage until help arrives.
- Treat the woman for shock.

Care of the mother

Clean her as best you can.

Place a sanitary towel, folded terry nappy or similar, between her legs.

Children's Problems

As children grow up there are a number of injuries and illnesses to which they are particularly prone. Some are directly related to the child's developing body which has yet to reach a state of adult maturity, e.g. greenstick fractures. Others occur because, during the child's early years, these illnesses commonly become apparent, e.g. asthma. With other illnesses, the body develops immunity after contact so that the adult years remain free of such problems, e.g. measles.

With younger children it is often difficult to gauge the nature and extent of their illness/injury. The child is unable to explain how he/she feels: 'I've got a tummy ache in my throat!' and the full effects of the illness/injury may be exaggerated to the extent of: 'My whole leg won't work!' following a small graze to the ankle. Don't despair – this is quite normal, and with patience, common sense and caution, it is not a problem.

When to Seek Medical Attention

- When the child remains unwell after 24 hours and is not improving.
- Has a headache associated with neck stiffness.
- Has a temperature of 38°C (100.4°F) and feels unwell.
- Has a temperature of 39°C (102.2°F).
- Has developed a skin rash.

The Child Needs to Go to Hospital If:

- He/she has a fit.
- You suspect a bone injury.
- The child has been, or may have been, knocked unconscious.
- The child has swallowed any poisons, tablets, household chemicals, etc.
- The child is difficult to rouse and makes little, or no, response to his/her parents.
- A cut may need stitching.

The above lists are not exhaustive and, as in all cases, common sense must be used when deciding if it is appropriate to seek medical advice.

The person in the best position to judge whether a child requires a medical opinion is often the parent or guardian, particularly when dealing with minor illness.

In some cases, professional advice can be sought from other sources; toddlers are often under the ongoing care of health visitors who are highly trained, specialist nurses. Illness or injury that occurs at school may be referred to a school nurse, if available.

Asthma

In recent years, the incidence of asthma in children (and adults) has increased considerably. This follows a high profile campaign aimed at doctors and other health professionals, making them more aware of asthma. Asthma is an illness that affects the muscles of the air passages in the lungs. They become constricted through spasm and make breathing out difficult. (See also p. 34.) As with adults, asthma can be triggered by allergy such as to a dog or cat, or by stress, but very often, there is no obvious cause.

A tendency towards frequent coughs requiring antibiotics may be the first indication to your family doctor that your child is asthmatic. Very often, doctors will now prescribe 'maintenance' therapy. This is the regular taking of asthma-relieving medication in preference to relying on medication taken at the time of an attack as the sole means of treatment.

You will notice • The child has difficulty in breathing, particularly in breathing out.

You may notice • The child is breathless and breathes at a faster rate than normal.

• The child breathes out with a wheezing sound.

• The child shows distress and anxiety, becoming restless and perhaps speaking with difficulty.

• The skin becomes dusky and the ear lobes and lips may become blue (cyanosis).

• The child becomes very tired and lethargic, taking rapid, but shallow, breaths. He/she may become unconscious.

Treatment

If the child becomes tired and lethargic, or shows any sign of dusky skin with blueness (cyanosis), dial 999 for an ambulance without delay.

Help the child to sit down in a comfortable position, if possible leaning forward on to a surface for support.

If there is medication to be taken during an asthma attack, help the child to take it or send for someone who can help.

Ensure that there is a good supply of fresh air to the child.

If there is quick improvement, allow the child to rest (with supervision) until he/she can resume normal activity.

If the asthma attack does not improve or, after initial improvement, becomes worse, you should seek medical advice without delay.

Inhalers

One of the most effective ways of delivering asthma-relieving medication is by inhaling it directly into the lungs where it has a near-immediate effect on the affected air passages. It is very difficult for children to manage the aerosol inhalers that would normally be used by teenagers and adults. Because of this, variants to the aerosol inhaler may be used and these include 'spacers'. The required dose of aerosol is put into one end of the 'spacer' and the child breathes normally (through the mouth) at the other end, thus receiving medication.

Parents of asthmatic children should discuss, with the family doctor, management of their child during an asthma attack while at an early stage in the child's treatment. This establishes the broad guidelines so that parents know when to call for medical assistance or summon an ambulance.

Croup

Very young children may be affected by croup. This is an alarming, but treatable condition caused by inflammation in the trachea (windpipe) and larynx (voice box). It often occurs at night and can recur after a short interval.

You will notice • The child's breathing is distressed.

You may notice • A hoarse voice.

- A cough that sounds like a rapid bark.
- A whistling noise as the child breathes in.
- In some cases, a dusky skin with blueness (cyanosis) to the ear lobes and lips.
- In severe cases, the way the child breathes will be affected. You will notice that as the child breathes in, the nostrils will flare, and the chest will seem to be tugged upward from the neck, with an associated shrugging of the shoulders.

Treatment

***In severe cases* Dial 999 for an ambulance without delay.**

Help the child to sit up and give plenty of reassurance.

Take the child into a steamy atmosphere to make breathing easier. This can be done by boiling water in the room or by running a hot water tap.

If an ambulance is not required, contact your own doctor.

After the croup attack has been relieved, keep the child in a steam-filled room to prevent recurrence.

Diabetes

Diabetes is a disease of the endocrine system. Parents may notice that their child is becoming lethargic, tires very easily and has to pass water frequently. When taken to the family doctor, diabetes may be diagnosed as the cause.

With diabetes, the pancreas fails to produce insulin so that the body's sugar levels are not controlled. Initially, the undiagnosed diabetic child will have too much sugar in the body: this is known as hyperglycaemia. This may be treated by injections of insulin. The problem, more commonly seen by first-aiders, is insufficient sugar (hypoglycaemia).

As with all chronic illnesses, the casualty will, in many cases, recognise the problem and direct first aid treatment. However, as the abnormal sugar levels affect the brain, the ability to think clearly and to take responsible action diminishes.

Hypoglycaemic attack (hypo) – Too little sugar

You may notice • A history of diabetes, with a rapid onset.

- A feeling of weakness or faintness.
- Shivering or muscle tremors.

- Awareness of own heart beating (palpitations).
- Strange or irrational behaviour and speech, even confusion and aggression.
- Cold, pale and clammy skin.
- Sweating.
- Strong-feeling pulse.
- Shallow breathing.
- Among the casualty's possessions you may find a diabetic warning card or SOS talisman, and an emergency supply of glucose.

TREATMENT

If the casualty is unconscious, check the ABC of Resuscitation (p. 6) and treat appropriately. The unconscious diabetic casualty will always require an ambulance.

If conscious, help the casualty to sit or lie down.

Give any sweet food or drink, e.g. milk, fizzy drink, small chocolate bar, sugar lumps, etc.

If there is improvement, repeat the above and allow the casualty to rest. If, after a further 15 minutes there is no improvement, repeat the above.

Ensure that the child's parents are aware of the event and advise them to seek medical advice as soon as possible.

Seek medical advice if the child is having frequent hypos or if you suspect other illness or infection.

Do not try to force food or drinks into a child who is unable to give full cooperation.

Hyperglycaemia – Too much sugar

You may notice • A history of diabetes, with rapid onset.

- A smell of acetone (nail varnish remover) on the breath.
- Dry skin.
- Rapid pulse.
- Deep, possibly laboured, breathing.
- Apparent slowness and lethargy.

TREATMENT

Sit or lie the casualty down.

Dial 999 for an ambulance.

Epiglottitis

This is much more serious than croup and is caused by inflammation of the epiglottis. This is a small piece of tissue that is located near to the airway in the throat. When it becomes inflamed, there is a possibility that the swelling may block off the windpipe. Epiglottitis is always a medical emergency. The symptoms may be very similar to croup but with the addition of a fever. It is also not restricted to very young children.

If you suspect that a child has epiglottitis, always dial 999 for an ambulance without delay.

You will notice • Distressed breathing.

- Fever.

You may notice • A hoarse voice.

- A cough that sounds like a rapid bark.
- A whistling noise on breathing in.
- In some cases, dusky skin with blueness (cyanosis) to the ear lobes and lips.
- In severe cases, the way the child breathes will be affected. You will notice that as the child breathes in, the nostrils

will flare and the chest will seem to be tugged upward from the neck, with an associated shrugging of the shoulders.

- Older children may sit bolt upright.
- Severe respiratory distress.

Treatment

Do not put your fingers, or allow the child to put its own fingers, into the mouth as this may stimulate the onset of spasm, blocking the airway completely.

Help the child to sit up and give support in this position.

Dial 999 for an ambulance.

Take the child into a steamy atmosphere so as to make breathing easier. This can be done by boiling water in the room or running a hot water tap.

Reassure the child.

Fever

Fever is a temperature raised beyond the normal body level of 37°C (98.4°F). Most commonly, it is caused by an infection such as chicken pox, measles, flu, etc. It can also be due to overheating through sunstroke.

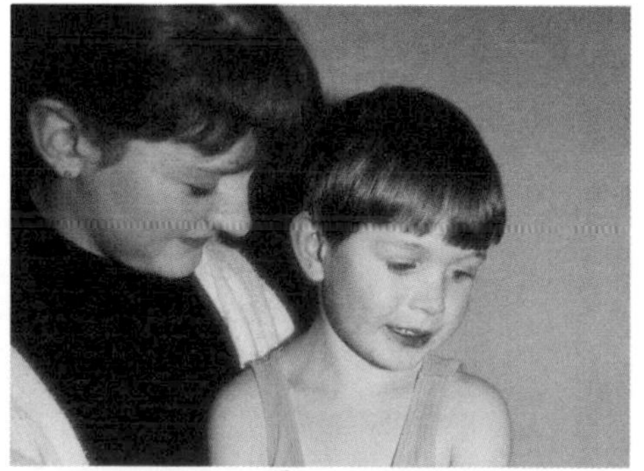

You will notice • A raised temperature.

You may notice • The child complains of feeling hot and/or cold.

- Flushed skin that is hot to touch.
- Sweating or dry skin.
- General aches and pains.
- Signs of illness, e.g. rash.

When to call a doctor

- ☐ The child's temperature is 38°C (100.4°F), and the child is unwell.
- ☐ The child's temperature is 39°C (102.2°F), whether or not unwell.

Treatment

Encourage the child to rest.

Cool the child by removing excess clothing and bedding.

Encourage the child to drink non-fizzy fluids, e.g. fresh fruit juice, water, unless the fever is associated with abdominal pains (he/she may need an operation).

Fits

Young children and infants can suffer from fits (convulsions) for a number of reasons. By far the most common cause is a very high temperature (fever), due to the young child's brain being less tolerant of variations in body temperature so that a fit (febrile convulsions) results. These fits should not be confused with temper tantrums.

Febrile convulsions

You will notice • That the child has a fever.

• That the child is very hot, has flushed skin and may be sweating.

• That the child is fitting: arched back, muscles twitching, jerking movements.

You may notice • The eyes rolling upward.

• The child's face may be blue if the breath is held.

• Dribbling/drooling at the mouth.

TREATMENT

Remove any covering and clothes.

Sponge the child with **tepid** water. Do this by starting at the head and regularly refresh the water in the sponge.

Prevent the child from hurting him/herself if the fit continues; place soft padding such as pillows around the child.

Do not try to restrain the child by force.

Once the fit stops, continue to cool the child.

If the child becomes unconscious, check the ABC of Resuscitation (p. 15 or p. 19) and treat appropriately.

Dial 999 for an ambulance.

> **DO NOT OVERCOOL THE CHILD** Once the fit has finished, cover the child with a light covering, e.g. a sheet.

Epilepsy

After febrile convulsions, epilepsy is the most common cause of fits in children. As with any other type of fit, the child must be seen by a doctor urgently if epilepsy has not been previously diagnosed. Epilepsy can occur in two basic forms: major (grand mal) and minor (petit mal).

Grand mal

This is the more alarming of the two types of epileptic fit.

You may notice • The child suddenly falls to the ground, sometimes crying out.

• The back arches and the body becomes stiff.

• The child's breathing may become distressed or stop (this is temporary).

• The child begins to fit: muscles twitching, jerking movements, noisy breathing, thrashing out with the limbs, grating of teeth.

• The child may wet or soil him/herself.

• As the fit finishes, the child gradually relaxes and wakes up after a few minutes but will initially be dazed and confused.

TREATMENT

Do not try to restrain the child physically.

Do not put your finger or any other object into the child's mouth.

Do not try to wake, or stimulate, the child before he/she starts to respond spontaneously.

Do not lift or move the child unless he/she is in danger.

Protect the child from injury with soft padding, e.g. pillows, rolled-up clothing.

When the fit stops, **gently** place the child in the recovery position (p. 23).

Stay with the child until he/she wakes.

Dial 999: If this is the child's first fit.

If the child has repeated fits.

If the child does not wake up after 5 minutes.

Petit mal

This can be very brief and, at times, can be mistaken for loss of concentration or day-dreaming. Recovery is spontaneous; the child may need reassurance.

You may notice • The child becomes trance-like.

• Slight twitching movements, even shuffling of the feet.

• Obscure movements, i.e. grinding of teeth, smacking of lips, rubbing the thumb against the fingers.

Foreskin Trapped in Zip

The foreskin of a young boy's penis tends to be rather fleshy and can be caught in the zip of his trousers, causing considerable pain and anxiety. Often, the foreskin will be bleeding.

Do not fiddle with the zip to try to release the foreskin!

Treatment

Apply cold compress to the trapped area without delay.

Take the boy to hospital with a cold compress in place.

Greenstick Fractures

Children's bones differ from those of adults in that they are more supple. Just as a young sapling, when bent, may split or crack rather than break, so it is for a child's arm and leg bones. For this reason, this type of break is known as a greenstick fracture.

Many injuries in younger children are difficult to assess as to whether there is any underlying greenstick fracture and so common sense must be used when a child has hurt an arm or leg. Unfortunately, it is not uncommon for parents to take their children (reluctantly) to a doctor or Accident Department some days after an injury because the child continues to 'make a fuss' whilst seemingly having normal or near normal movement – only to find that on X-ray there is a greenstick fracture.

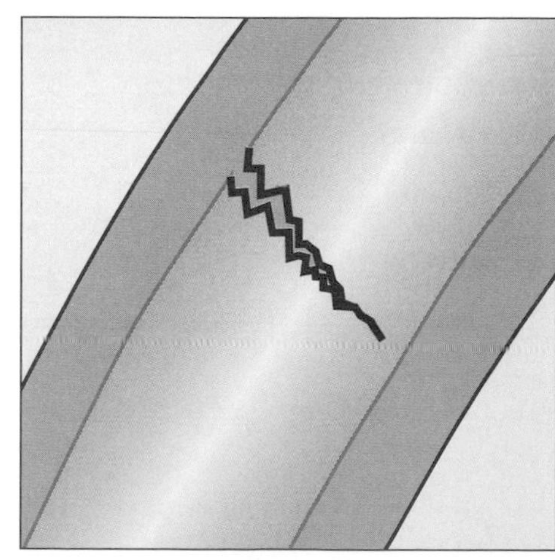

You may notice • A recent history of an injury to the affected part.

• Localised pain or discomfort.

• Swelling and redness (bruising after some hours).

• Reluctance to use the injured part.

TREATMENT

Immobilise the injured part if necessary, to prevent pain with movement.

Arrange for the child to go to the hospital's Accident Department. It may not be necessary to call an ambulance; common sense should be used.

Sunburn

Children's skin is extremely sensitive to exposure to the sun. Whereas fair-haired or fair-skinned children are particularly sensitive, care must be taken with all children. Golden brown skin after sun bathing is rightly called sun**burn.** (See p. 137.)

You may notice • Redness of the skin.

• Associated itching or pain.

• Tenderness.

• Blistering.

TREATMENT

If there is blistering or skin damage, seek medical advice. ***Do not*** burst any blisters.

Cool the area by sponging with cold water.

Use calamine lotion or after-sun lotion to provide continued cooling.

If the tenderness causes distress, give the child the recommended dose of paracetamol syrup.

Sunstroke

This can occur very suddenly and may follow a period where the child feels unwell and restless. Young children, in particular, are prone to sunstroke as they are unable to control their body temperature as well as adults (see also p. 114).

You may notice • The child complains of a headache and feeling unwell.

• Sunburn.

• Restlessness and, possibly, confusion.

• Flushed skin that is hot and dry.

• Full 'bounding' pulse.

• Sudden deterioration, even collapse.

TREATMENT

Move the child to a cool place.

Remove clothing and wrap the child in a cold, wet sheet until the extreme hotness of the skin has declined.

Replace the wet sheet with a dry one and allow the child to rest.

Seek medical advice if the child does not make a rapid recovery.

IF UNCONSCIOUS

- Check the ABC of Resuscitation (p. 15 or p. 19) and treat as appropriate.
- Dial 999 for an ambulance.

Swallowed and Inhaled Foreign Bodies

Unusual objects taken into the mouth (and nose) have three potential routes to travel:

Swallowed – into the stomach.

Inhaled – into the windpipe, lower air passages and lungs.

Out – of the mouth/nose.

Small children are very poor historians, unable to recall with clarity whether they have taken in any objects, in what quantities and when. This is due, in part, to their fear and in response to their parents' anxiety as well as their age.

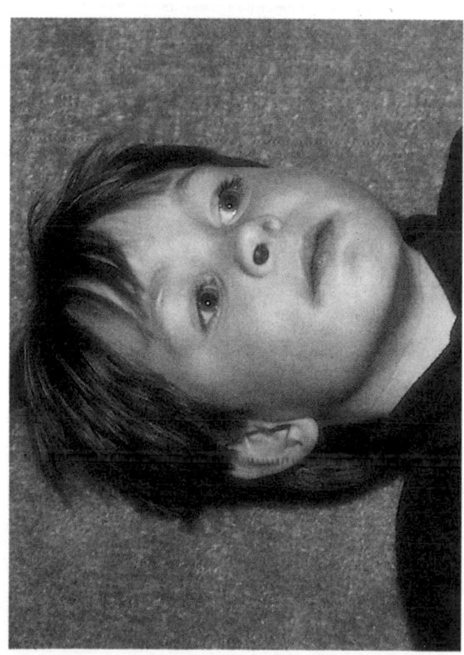

Dos and Don'ts

- ☐ ***Do not*** try to make the child sick.
- ☐ ***Do*** keep the child calm. Moreover, keep calm yourself.

Often, it is impossible for the parent of a toddler or young child to be sure of what exactly has happened. If you suspect that a child has swallowed or inhaled something then you must seek medical advice.

Treatment

If the child is unconscious: check the ABC of Resuscitation (p. 19) and act appropriately.

If the child is conscious: keep calm and try to identify what the child has taken, how much was taken and when it was taken. If this information is not forthcoming from the child, ask other children who may be present, but do not force the issue. If the child has breathing difficulties, always assume the object has been inhaled and treat as for choking (p. 88).

> If the child may have swallowed berries, etc, take a sample with you to the hospital.

Dial 999 for an ambulance if the object is sharp, or large, or has caused burning to the mouth or if there are any signs of breathing difficulties. Otherwise, take the child to hospital.

Foreign Bodies in Other Orifices

These will need removal by a doctor. If the child is in pain rather than being just upset, dial 999 for an ambulance, otherwise take the child to hospital by whatever means available.

Trapped Fingers

This is probably one of the most common minor injuries that occurs to toddlers and young children. Fortunately, in most cases, there is little likelihood of damage beyond the immediate pain and discomfort.

Treatment

Carefully examine the affected parts and look for any cuts or signs of bone injury. If present, treat as appropriate (see p. 55).

If there is no obvious injury, bathe the affected area in cold water (or, if the child will let you, use a cold compress) until the pain subsides.

Cold compress

Either:

- Crush some ice cubes in a plastic bag which is, in turn, wrapped in a towel or similar.

Or:

- Use a towel to wrap around a bag of frozen vegetables (such as peas).
- Do not allow the ice to come into direct contact with the child's skin.

Travel Sickness

Travel sickness is usually brought about by the balance mechanism of the inner ear being sensitive to movement, particularly when the child cannot see out of the windows so that the movement is not associated with his/her surroundings. Sometimes, too, there is a psychological aspect to travel sickness. If the parents are very anxious because they expect their child to be travel sick – then travel sick that child will be! Do not allow the child to become too hot; do not give the child fizzy drinks prior to, or during, a journey, or a full meal.

Treatment

If the child feels sick, open the windows to give fresh air and encourage the child to take deep breaths. If possible stop the vehicle to allow the child to rest and recover.

Medical advice

For some children, travel sickness is a frequent problem that can affect even the shortest of journeys. In these cases, or when undertaking an unusually long journey with a child who tends towards travel sickness, it is advisable to seek advice from your family doctor.

Common infectious diseases of childhood

These are technically beyond the realm of first aid but it is useful to provide an easy reference chart.

	Signs and Symptoms	Incubation period after contact	Isolation period	Nursing and treatment
CHICKEN POX *(Varicella)*	May start with a cold, headache or sickness. High temperature. Small red pimples (first on body then on face and limbs) which turn into yellow blisters, then break.	10 – 20 days	2 days after last spots appear, or when scabs have fallen off	Bed rest. Relieve itching with calomine lotion. Try to stop child scratching (little ones may need cotton mittens) to prevent further infection and scars (pock marks). Keep child's nails short and clean.
GERMAN MEASLES *(Rubella)*	Slight temperature or sore throat. Swollen tender glands at back of neck. Flat pink spots spreading into blotches.	12 – 21 days	7 days after rash appears	Rest in bed or on sofa in warm room for 2 or 3 days.
MEASLES *(Morbilli)*	Loss of appetite. High temperature. Sneezing, running nose, dry cough. Watery, pink eyes. Blotchy pink spots on neck, forehead and cheeks, spreading to body later.	10 – 15 days	7 – 10 days after rash appears	Bed rest until 3 days after temperature falls (about 7 days altogether). Sleep and plenty to drink. Shield eyes from strong light.
MUMPS *(Epidemic Parotitis)*	Swelling below ear spreading to face or neck. Pain when chewing or swallowing. No rash.	17 – 21 days	7 days after swelling subsides	Rest in bed. Relieve pain with paracetamol syrup or whatever doctor prescribes. Bland food and drinks (e.g. rosehip syrup) avoiding sharp-tasting fruit drinks like orange and lemon.
SCARLET FEVER *(Scarlatina)*	Sore, reddened throat and tongue. High temperature and vomiting. Head and stomach pains. Small red spots, flushed skin, usually starting on back, armpits or groin.	2 – 5 days	7 – 10 days	Rest in bed. Call the family doctor.
WHOOPING COUGH *(Pertussis)*	Starts as an ordinary cold. Dry repeated cough with 'whooping' sound as breath is drawn in. Vomiting. No rash.	1 – 3 weeks	At least 2 weeks after coughing stops	Call the family doctor.

Choking

Anything that lodges at the back of the throat, or within the windpipe, will cause the casualty to choke. The back of the throat is a very sensitive area that, if stimulated by a first aider trying to remove an object with the fingers, may cause the top of the windpipe to close completely through muscle spasm.

The treatment for choking has been recently revised and the methods used for small children and babies vary from those used for adults.

You will notice • Difficulty in speaking and crying.

• Difficulty in breathing.

• Acute anxiety.

You may notice • Inability to speak or to make any other sound.

• The casualty grasps the front of the neck, or points to the mouth and throat.

• The casualty becomes blue.

Choking in small children and babies

Position the child or baby so that the head is lower than the trunk.

> Sit and hold the child or baby face down, resting your forearm while supporting the head by firmly holding the jaw. Your arm should rest on your thigh for additional support.

Give 5 sharp slaps between the child's or baby's shoulder-blades. Use the flat of your hand.

Check to see if any obstruction has come up into the mouth.

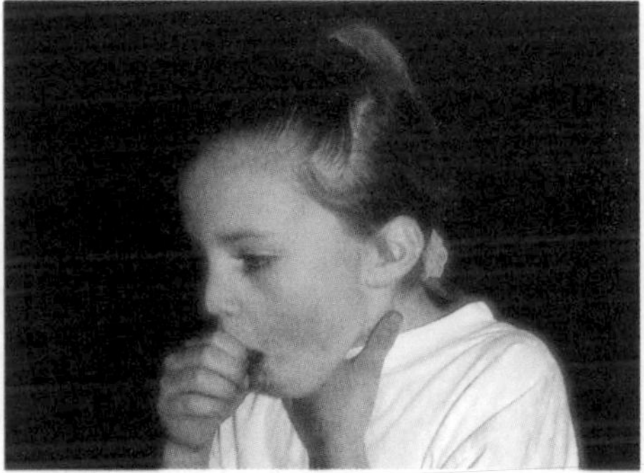

If the backslaps fail, you will need to give up to 5 chest thrusts.

Turn the child or baby on to its back.

For a child: use the first and second finger of one hand, to find the position where the lower ribs meet the abdomen. Now slide your fingers up the line of the ribs to the notch where the ribs meet the breastbone. Place one finger in the notch and the other next to the first finger, on the breastbone (p. 21).

Place the heel of the other hand on to the breastbone immediately next to the fingers; this is the place at which you will press down.

For a baby: lay the baby along your thighs with its head nearest your knee.

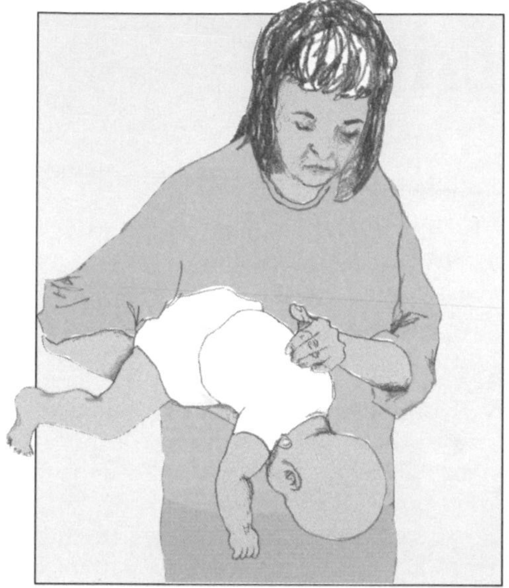

Draw an imaginary line between the baby's nipples. Place two fingers from your free hand on the breastbone approximately one finger's breadth below this imaginary line (this is where you will do the chest thrusts). (see illustration p. 17).

Give 5 rapid downward chest thrusts.

If the obstruction has not moved, alternate between 5 backslaps and 5 chest thrusts.

Do not use the abdominal thrust (Heimlich Manoeuvre) on a baby or small child. You may cause severe damage to the abdominal organs, e.g. tear the liver.

If the child or baby becomes unconscious, dial 999 for an ambulance.

Give artificial ventilation to try to blow the obstruction farther down the baby's or child's airways so that air can enter one of the lungs (see pp. 16 and 20).

If not breathing, alternate 5 breaths of artificial ventilation with 5 backslaps and 5 chest thrusts until help arrives or the blockage clears.

Choking in adults and older children

Position the casualty so that the head is lower than the trunk.

Give 5 sharp slaps between the casualty's shoulder-blades, using the flat of your hand. Check to see if the obstruction has come up into the mouth.

If the backslaps fail, you will need to give up to 5 abdominal thrusts (Heimlich Manoeuvre).

Do this by standing behind the casualty and encircling his/her waist with your arms. Grasp your hands together in the upper part of the casualty's abdomen and pull upwards under the ribs sharply; do this 5 times. Check to see if the obstruction has come up into the mouth.

If the obstruction has not moved, alternate between 5 backslaps and 5 abdominal thrusts.

If the casualty becomes unconscious dial 999 for an ambulance.

If not breathing, alternate 5 breaths of artificial ventilation with 5 backslaps and 5 chest thrusts until help arrives or the blockage clears.

To carry out abdominal thrusts on the unconscious casualty, lay the casualty on his/her back, kneel astride the upper thighs and join your hands together until your arms are locked straight on to the casualty's upper abdomen. Push upwards under the ribs; repeat 5 times.

Confusion

Confusion – the loss of rational thought and action – is a symptom of many different illnesses and injuries. It may be severe, being instantly recognisable, or it can be more discreet.

Possible causes of confusion:

Stroke.

Diabetes.

Following a fit.

Hypothermia.

Lack of oxygen (hypoxia).

Infection.

Shock.

Head injury.

Undiagnosed illness.

Effect of prescribed medication.

Substance abuse.

Drunkenness.

A WORD OF WARNING

- In many cases, an unwell person who exhibits confusion is mistakenly assumed to be drunk. Never jump to this conclusion. Always be aware that such a casualty may be ill and need medical assistance.
- Do not forget, even if drunk, the casualty may also be diabetic, having a stroke or being ill in some other way.

Making a diagnosis

On many occasions, as a first aider, you will find a casualty in circumstances that suggest they have been injured, or they are with someone who will tell you that the casualty has been unwell.

NOT SURE IF SOMEONE IS ILL?

- Confusion is not normal. If help is not sought, ongoing confusion may lead to the casualty inflicting self-injury or, on rare occasions, injuring others.
- If you are not sure – seek medical advice.

EXAMINATION	POINT OF NOTE	POSSIBLE CAUSE
Head and face	Bruising Possible fractures	Head injury
Eyes	Pupils unequal in size Pupil reaction to light slow	Head injury
Breath	Acetone (nail varnish smell) Alcohol	Diabetes Drunk
Whole body	Very hot, with a rapid pulse Very cold, with a slow pulse Pale, cold and clammy, with a rapid pulse Weakness in one or more of the limbs	Infection Hypothermia Shock Stroke
Speech	Slurred Disjointed or wrong words being used	Stroke After a fit Drunk Stroke Drugs
Understanding	Seemingly unable to understand	Does not understand language Stroke Head injury
Colour	Flushed face with slow, strong pulse	Head injury Stroke Heatstroke

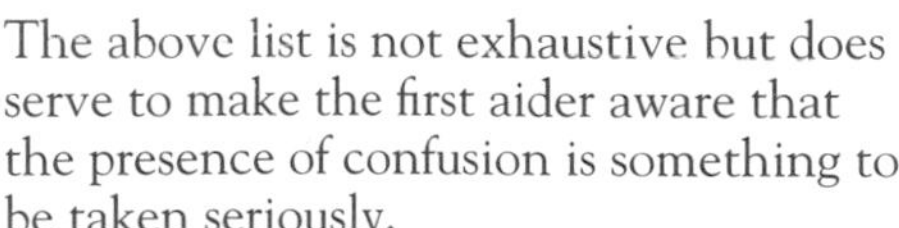

The above list is not exhaustive but does serve to make the first aider aware that the presence of confusion is something to be taken seriously.

Dealing with the confused casualty

In many cases, the confused casualty is easily managed with kind words, plenty of reassurance and non-threatening behaviour. Remember: a casualty, even though confused, is not necessarily unaware of the surroundings and what is happening. In many cases, the individual will feel afraid.

The casualty who is uncooperative may respond to a calm and reasoned approach. Never try to force him/her to do anything unwillingly. Even if help is refused, it is always worth phoning for an ambulance so that professional help can more fully assess the casualty and act as needed.

Cramps

A cramp is a sudden and painful episode of muscle spasm. It can occur during exercise as a result of excessive sweating or, very often, while asleep.

You will notice • Complaint of sudden pain within a muscle.

You may notice • Limited movement and limb use.

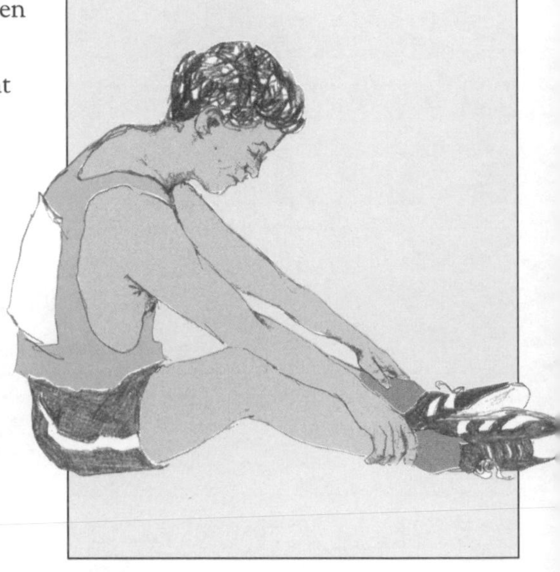

Treatment Summary

The general principles are to relieve the spasm and help the casualty to regain normal movement.

Cramp in the thigh

For cramp in the back of the thigh, gently straighten the casualty's knee.

For cramp in the front of the thigh, gently bend the leg at the knee.

Massage the affected muscle firmly until the pain has been relieved.

Cramp in the lower leg

Straighten the casualty's knee.

Draw the casualty's foot up toward the shin.

Massage the muscles until the pain is relieved.

Cramp in the foot

Get the casualty to put weight on the affected foot; this can be done either by pushing the foot firmly against your hand or by getting the casualty to stand.

When the worst of the pain has diminished, massage the foot, concentrating particularly on the underside.

Use of cold or heat

Cramps can be greatly relieved by the use of cold (or heat).

Wrap a bag of frozen vegetables in a towel and apply to the affected area.

Or place a covered hot water bottle on to the affected area.

Seeking medical advice

If the cramps are persistent, particularly if they are not associated with exercise, you should seek advice from your doctor.

Stitches

A stitch is a form of cramp that occurs due to low oxygen levels in the muscles of the abdomen. As the muscles become fatigued during exercise, pain occurs.

Treatment

Stop the casualty exercising.

If necessary, sit the casualty down.

The stitch will go within a few minutes.

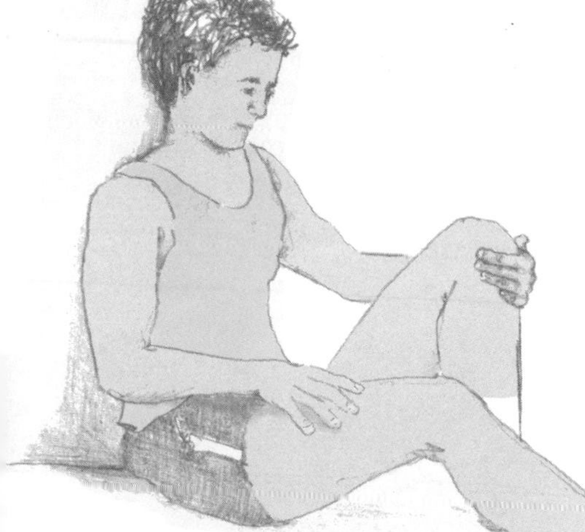

Stiff neck

When the muscles around the neck go into spasm, the casualty is said to have a stiff neck. The condition is most commonly related to poor posture.

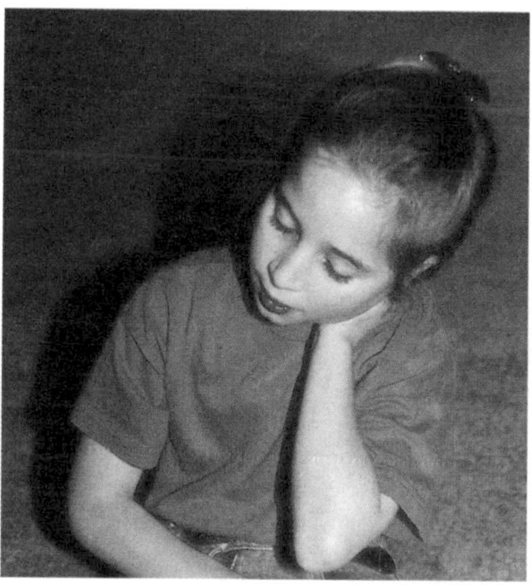

You may notice • The casualty's head is inclined to one side.

If accompanied by fever and headache call your doctor.

Treatment

Ask the casualty to 'roll' the head so that the affected side is stretched.

If the pain is severe, apply a cold compress or a covered hot water bottle.

Massage the affected area.

Diabetes

With diabetes, the body cannot control the sugar levels within the blood. Normally, the pancreas produces insulin which controls the blood's level of sugar. This is not so with diabetes. Diabetics are prone to two main problems - hypoglycaemia and hyperglycaemia (see also Diabetes in Children, p. 80).

Hypoglycaemia

More commonly known as 'hypo', this is the most common diabetic problem encountered by a first aider. For whatever reason – illness, exercise or missing a meal – blood sugar levels drop to a degree where the functioning of the brain is affected. This can occur with very little warning. As the attack progresses, the casualty may become disorientated and unable to recognise what is happening.

You may notice • The casualty (or another person) tells you he/she is diabetic and having a 'hypo'.

- Weakness and faintness.
- Muscle tremors.
- Palpitations.
- Pale, cold and clammy skin.
- A 'bounding' pulse.
- Uncharacteristic behaviour, confusion, aggression, even denial there is anything wrong!
- Gradual drowsiness, even to the point of collapse and unconsciousness.
- Breathing may become shallow.
- The casualty may be wearing a bracelet or locket or be carrying a warning card informing you of the condition.

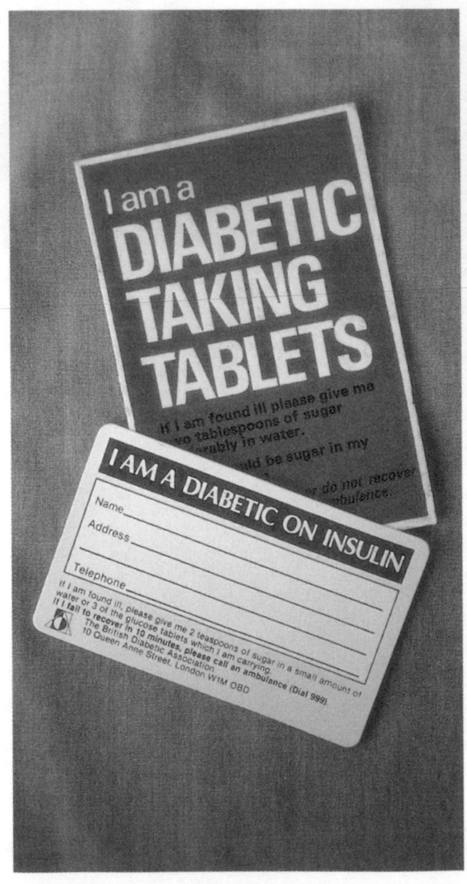

Unconscious diabetic

- ☐ Do not try to force food or drink into the casualty's mouth.
- ☐ Check the ABC of Resuscitation (p. 6) and respond appropriately.
- ☐ Dial 999 for an ambulance.

Treatment

Suggest that the casualty rests, either by sitting or lying down.

Give the casualty a sweet drink, glucose sweets, sugar lumps or chocolate.

Provided the casualty's condition improves quickly, give more sweet food or drink.

Once the casualty feels better, allow to rest until fully recovered.

If the casualty does not improve or gives cause for concern, dial 999.

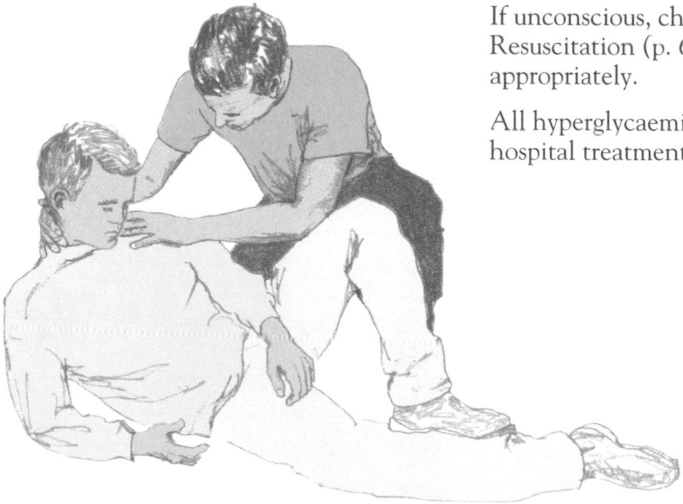

Hyperglycaemia

In this situation, the blood sugar level has become too high. This usually occurs over many hours and if not treated, will lead to coma.

You may notice • The casualty (or another person) tells you that he/she is diabetic.

• Breath may smell of acetone (nail varnish remover).

• Dry skin.

• Rapid pulse.

• Difficulty in breathing.

• Disorientation or confusion.

• Drowsiness to the point of collapse and unconsciousness.

• The casualty may be wearing a bracelet or locket or carrying a warning card, informing you of the condition.

Treatment

If unconscious, check the ABC of Resuscitation (p. 6) and respond appropriately.

All hyperglycaemic casualties need hospital treatment – dial 999.

Drowning

Help for a victim of drowning may be hazardous to the first aider as, in many cases, rescue from the water is first necessary. Apart from the dangers of an uncooperative and struggling casualty who may render the potential rescuer in need of urgent rescue from drowning, there are other hazards.

Open water can be cold, even during the summer months. Temperatures in the range of 3°-15°C (37°-59°F) are common, with inland waterways in some countries freezing at times during the winter. Normal body temperature is 37°C (98.4°F) so a considerable drop in body temperature can occur following immersion.

Dangers

Even a strong swimmer may be unable to swim due to the effects of cold.

Uncontrollable gasping on entering cold water, which may lead to inhalation of water.

Heart attack due to a sudden rise in blood pressure.

Onset of hypothermia which causes lethargy so that the victim is slow to recognise danger.

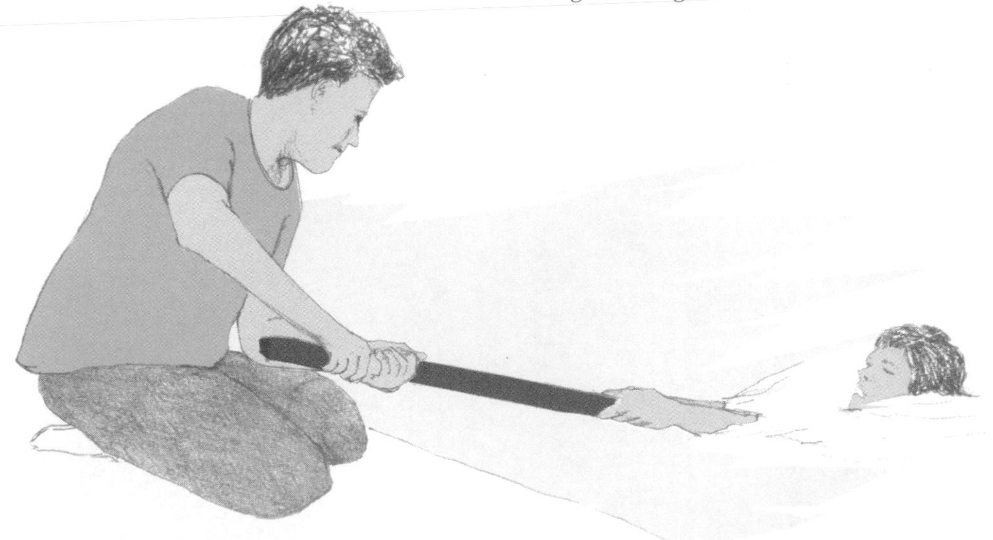

Drowning in the home

Any pool of water is a potential hazard to toddlers and young children. Drownings can even occur in 2-3 in (5-7cm) of water. Obvious risk areas are the bath, paddling pools, fish ponds and water barrels.

Drowning explained

Very few people drown because their lungs fill with water. As water enters the casualty's throat, the muscles clamp shut. Water continues to enter the casualty's stomach and this can cause a problem if it is inhaled following rescue.

DOS AND DON'TS OF RESCUE FROM WATER

- ***Don't*** enter the water yourself unless absolutely necessary.
- ***Do*** send for any professional help that is rapidly available in the area, e.g. lifeguards, beach officers.
- ***Don't*** try to tow the casualty (unless you are a trained person).
- ***Do*** stay on land. ***Wade*** to a safe depth (i.e. top of thighs) and throw a rescue ring or rope, or try to reach the casualty with a stick or similar.

When the casualty has been rescued

Check the ABC of Resuscitation, see p. 12 (adults), p. 18 (babies) or p. 22 (children) and act appropriately.

Do not attempt to pump any water from the casualty's lungs or stomach.

Keep the casualty (and rescuers who have entered the water) warm, wrap them in blankets/clothing.

Dial 999 for an ambulance.

CPR

A victim of drowning may require a slower rate of CPR. This is because the lungs become temporarily less elastic and inflations become less easy to achieve and will take longer.

Any victim of drowning, even if seemingly fully recovered, must go to hospital.

Ear Problems

The ear can be prone to a number of problems. By far the most common are infection and foreign bodies being put into the ear. Others range from boils in the ear to a ruptured ear drum.

DISCHARGES FROM THE EAR

- Medical advice must be sought if there is a discharge or bleeding from the ear.
- If the discharge is thin, watery and stained red, always suspect a fractured skull (p. 111).

Bleeding from the ear

This may have numerous causes, e.g. ruptured ear drum, a foreign body pushed deep into the ear or a blow to the head.

You will notice • Bleeding from the ear.

You may notice • The casualty complains of a sharp pain within the ear.

• The casualty is deaf on the affected side.

TREATMENT

Do not plug the ear.

Sit or lay the casualty down and incline the head toward the affected side.

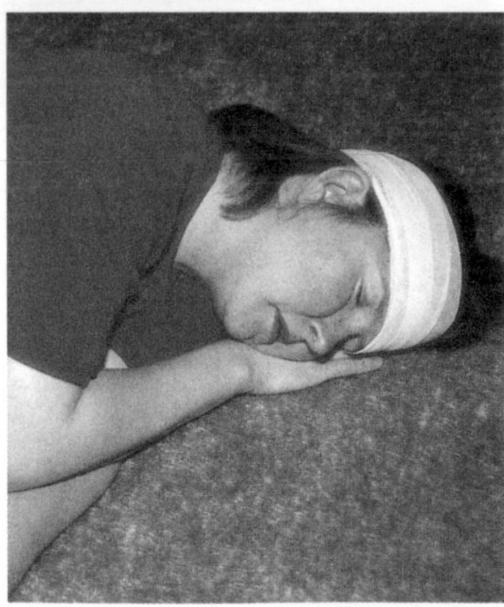

Cover the ear with a sterile dressing (or similar).

Arrange for the casualty to go to hospital (keeping the head inclined).

Earache

This is particularly common among children suffering from a middle ear infection. It can also be caused by a boil, a dental problem, a foreign body within the ear or during or after flying.

Treatment

If there is a discharge from the ear, a raised temperature or loss of hearing, it is essential that you seek medical advice immediately.

If the ear is throbbing and there are none of the above symptoms, advise the casualty to take the recommended dose of a simple painkiller such as paracetamol (children should take paracetamol syrup).

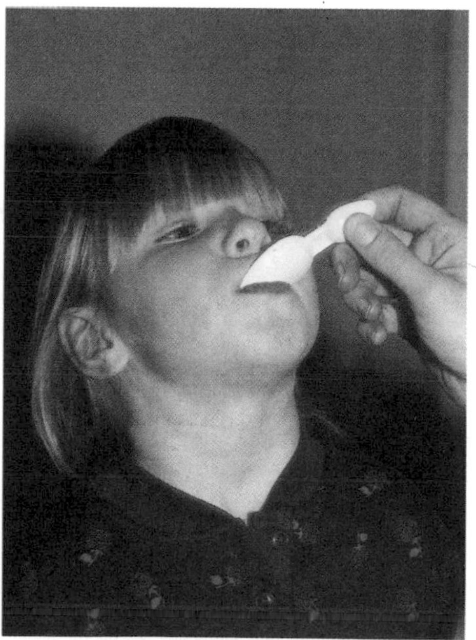

Place a covered hot water bottle against the ear.

If the pain continues, or you have any concerns, seek medical advice.

Foreign bodies in the ear

Children may push an object into the ear and this can damage the ear drum. Insects can fly or crawl into the ear.

Foreign bodies that have been pushed into the ear

- ☐ These may become stuck within the ear canal. Such objects should always be removed by a doctor.

Treatment for insects in the ear

Sit the casualty down and incline the head, with the affected ear uppermost.

Using tepid water, gently flood the affected ear until the insect floats out.

Take the casualty to hospital if you are unable to float the insect out.

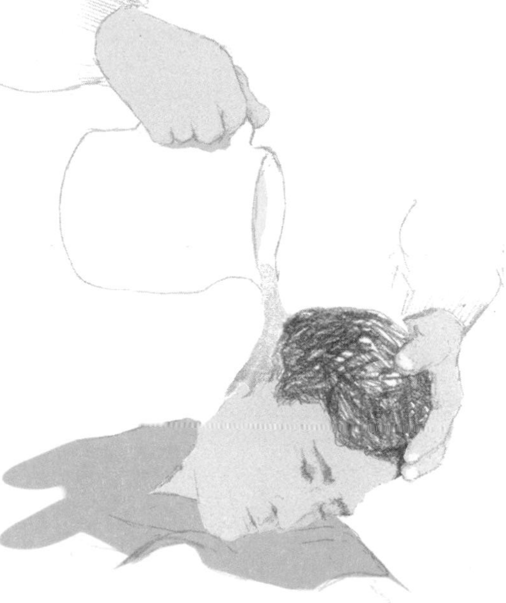

Eye Problems

The eye is a very delicate organ. If scarring occurs on the surface of the eye, blindness may result. The eye can become sore for a number of reasons, and it is important for the first aider to be able to recognise when it is necessary to seek medical aid.

SEEK MEDICAL AID

- When there is a cut to the surface of the eye.
- When the eye has been burned.
- When the eye has a discharge.
- If you suspect an infection.
- When an object is embedded in the eye.

Eye Infection

You will notice • Complaint of a sore eye.

You may notice • Complaint of a gritty sensation, pain on blinking and other eye movements.

- The eye and eyelids may be inflamed.
- The eyelids may be warm to touch.
- The eye may be watering.
- The eye may be discharging.
- Blurred vision.

TREATMENT

Prevent the casualty making the condition worse by rubbing the eyes.

Ensure the casualty receives medical help.

Do not cover the eye as this will increase the rate of germs multiplying.

Contact lens problems

Contact lenses come in two main varieties: hard and soft. The hard type are fairly small and firm whereas the soft types are comparatively large and relatively floppy.

Most wearers of contact lenses become very adept at managing their own eye care, including any problems that might occur.

Displaced contact lens

The eye is a very smooth rounded organ and, on occasions, a contact lens becomes displaced from over the pupil to another part of the eye, causing varying measures of irritation.

TREATMENT

Assist the casualty to locate the lens. Do this by gently sliding the upper eyelid up and over the top of the eye and ask the casualty to look up, down, left and right. If necessary, repeat this with the bottom eyelid. **Remember** the casualty will usually be very adept at doing this.

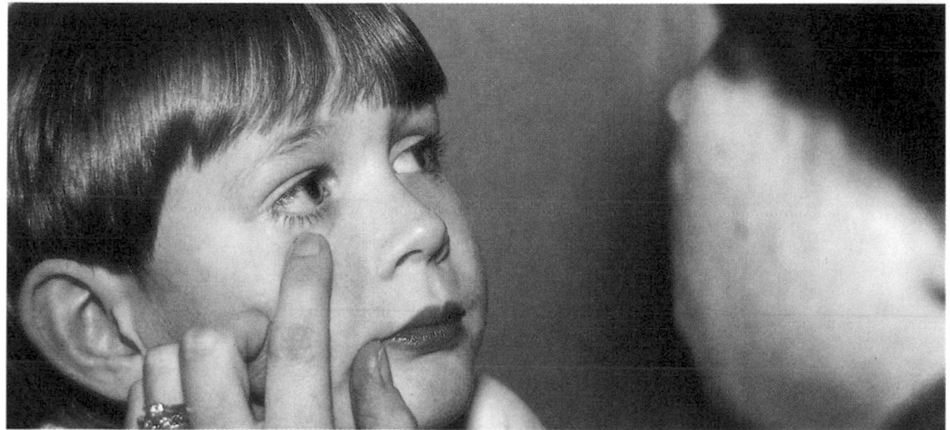

When the lens is located, gently try to massage it back into a normal position. Do this by working over the closed eyelid, asking the casualty to keep the eye still.

If unsuccessful, refer the casualty to an optician or seek medical advice.

Other foreign bodies

Prevent the casualty rubbing his/her eyes.

Sit the casualty down in a good light.

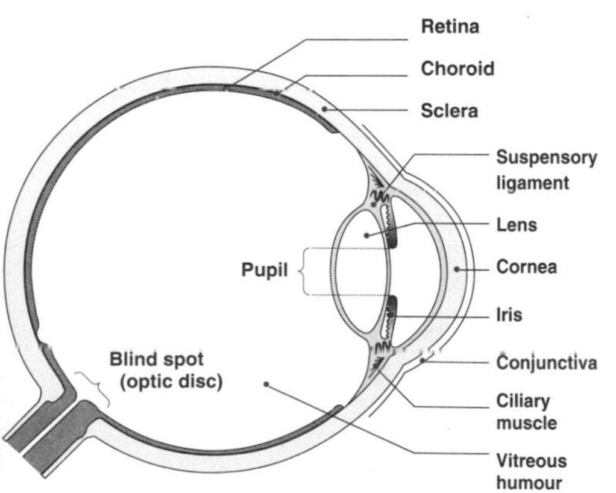

Examine the eye for any sign of the foreign body. Do this by gently sliding the upper eyelid up and over the top of his eye, asking the casualty to look up, down, left and right. If necessary, repeat this with the bottom eyelid.

If you can see a foreign body, you will need to 'float' it out.

Ask the casualty to incline the head on to the affected side; place a towel (or similar) over the shoulder on that side.

Using a cup of clean water, slowly pour it into the corner of the eye next to the nose.

Do not pour the water directly on to the coloured part of the area.

As the water runs across the eye it should 'float' the foreign body out.

If this is unsuccessful, and provided you are sure that the foreign body is not sticking to, or penetrating, the eye, use a moist swab or the damp corner of a clean handkerchief to lift it off the eye.

If the foreign body remains on the eye, or if the casualty is experiencing undue discomfort, abandon your efforts and obtain expert help from a local doctor or hospital.

Burns to the eye

Splashes of certain substances into the eye can cause a chemical or heat burn which, in turn, may lead to scarring and blindness.

You will notice • The casualty tells you something has splashed into the eye.

You may notice • Extreme pain in the eye.

• Redness and swelling in, and around, the eye.

• Watering of the eye.

• Inability to open the eye.

Treatment

Prevent the casualty rubbing, or touching, the eye.

Flood the eye with running water from a gently running tap, or by continually pouring water from a glass or jug.

Warning!

- Ensure that in washing out the eye you do not allow eyewash from the affected eye to enter and contaminate the unaffected eye. Suitably protect your hands and, as far as possible, the casualty's face from becoming contaminated by chemicals.

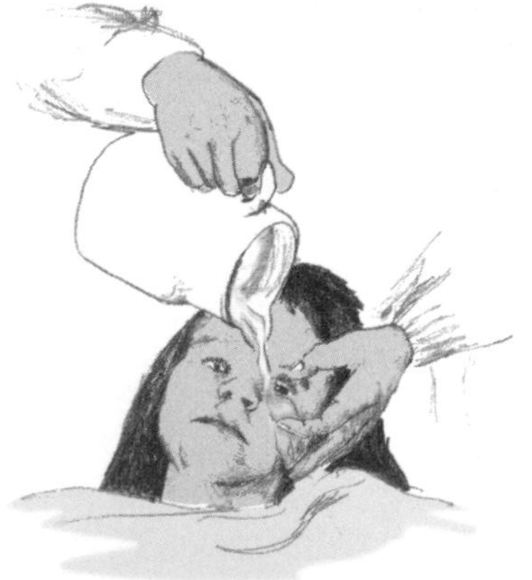

Dial 999 for an ambulance.

Continue to flood the eye until the ambulance arrives.

Flash burns ("Arc eye")

These occur when the eye is exposed to excessive glare produced by reflection of the sun's rays from a surface such as snow, etc. It can also be caused by looking into intense light produced by a welding torch.

You will notice • Extreme pain in the eyes.

You may notice • Sensitivity to light.

• Poor, blurred visibility.

• Redness and watering of the eyes.

Treatment

Apply eye pads to both eyes.

Take, or send, the casualty to hospital.

Faints

A faint is a brief collapse involving loss of consciousness. It is caused by a reduction in the blood flow to the brain. Fainting can be a reaction to shock, pain or lack of food. Most commonly, however, it occurs when someone is inactive for a prolonged period, such as through standing still, and a significant amount of blood pools in the legs, thus reducing the flow to the brain.

A faint is a minor event but, on occasions, the casualty may injure him/herself when falling.

You will notice • The casualty collapses and is unconscious.

- The pulse is very slow.
- The skin is very pale.

You may notice • Complaint of faintness or dizziness.

TREATMENT

If you were not with the casualty who has apparently fainted, always check the ABC of Resuscitation (p. 6).

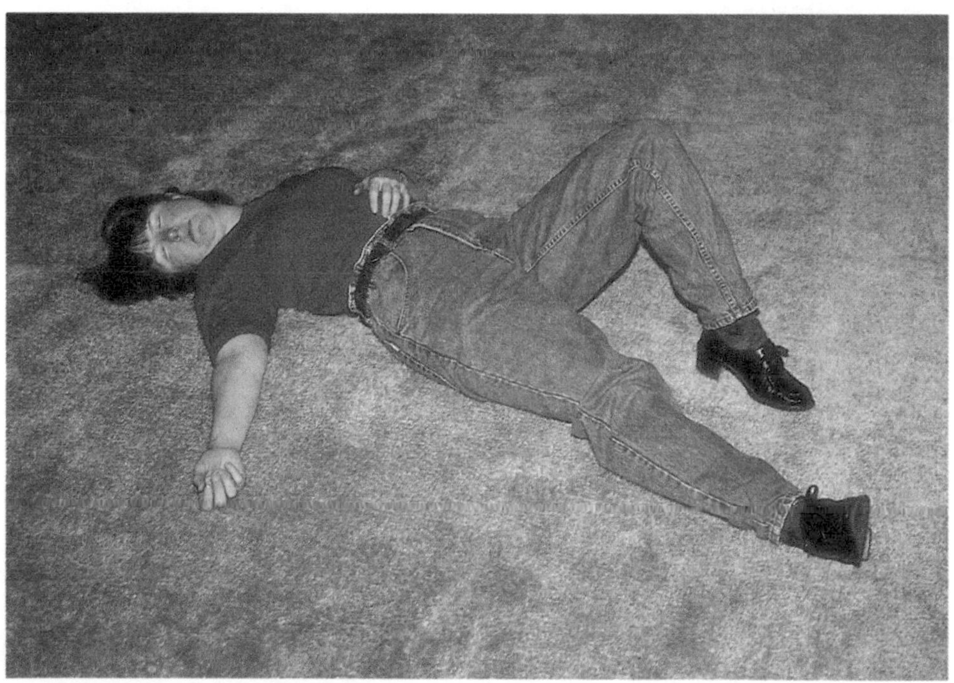

Raise the casualty's legs; use a chair or ask a bystander to give support.

Loosen tight clothing at the neck, chest and waist.

Reassure the casualty and encourage to stay lying down until fully recovered.

Gradually help the casualty to sit and then to stand up.

If still unconscious after a couple of minutes, turn the casualty into the recovery position (p. 8) and dial 999 for an ambulance.

Someone who feels faint

You will notice • Very pale appearance.

• Complaint of faintness or giddiness.

TREATMENT

Sit the casualty down.

Ask the casualty to put head between his/her legs.

Loosen any tight clothing at the neck, chest and waist.

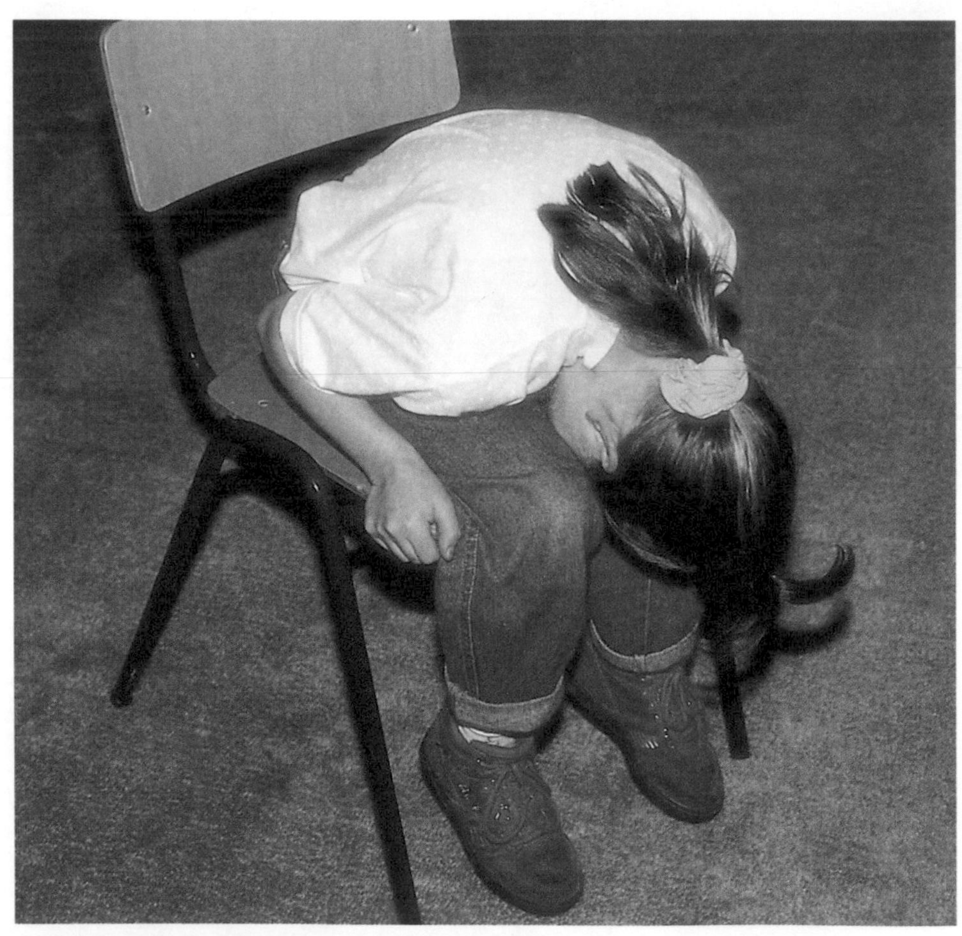

Fever

A fever is when the body's temperature becomes raised beyond its normal level of 37°C (98.4°F). This is usually due to the presence of an infection (bacterial or viral). In response to the infection, the body 'works harder' to maintain its equilibrium and to fight the infection – this causes a rise in body temperature.

Taking temperatures

There are a number of alternative methods of taking a temperature:

Fever strip

This is a small strip which is placed on the forehead. The body's temperature activates a colour change.

Under the arm

This requires a mercury (glass rod) or digital thermometer, the bulb being placed into the armpit and the arm held tight to the body. When taking a temperature by this method, the thermometer should be left in place for 3 minutes.

Both the above methods measure the outer temperature of the body which will be less than the internal temperature by about 1°C, i.e. 38°C (100.4°F) instead of 39°C (102.2°F).

By mouth

This requires a mercury or digital thermometer, the bulb being placed under the tongue. When taking a temperature by this method, the thermometer should be left in place for 2 minutes.

In the back passage

This requires a mercury thermometer specifically designed for this purpose. Shop-bought rectal thermometers have a blue bulb (rather than the normal silver). The thermometer must be lubricated with Vaseline and the bulb inserted only 1-1½ in (2-4 cm). When taking a temperature by this method, obtain expert help and keep the thermometer in place for 2 minutes.

False readings

These can be obtained if the mercury thermometer is stored in a warm place and is not shaken down prior to use. Also, if the person has just had a cold or warm drink, the temperature, when taken by mouth, will be false. Always wait 15-20 minutes after the casualty has completed a drink (or meal). The same time limit should apply if you are taking the external temperature after the casualty has just had a bath, or has been sitting in front of a fan.

Celsius/Fahrenheit

- Normal 37°C = 98.4°F
- 38°C = 100.4°F
- 39°C = 102.2°F
- 40°C = 104.0°F

Which method to use

When someone seems unwell, it is important to measure the temperature accurately.

Casualty	Routine check	When very poorly
Baby	Fever strip	Under the arm
Child	Under the arm	In the back passage (with expert help)
Adult	By mouth	By mouth

Never take a baby or child's temperature by putting a thermometer in its mouth.

When to call a doctor

Anyone who feels unwell and has a temperature of 38°C (100.4°F), should seek medical advice. Anyone with a temperature of 39°C (102.2°F) should **always** seek medical advice.

Treatment

Encourage the casualty to rest.

Encourage the casualty to drink plenty of fluids (avoid fizzy drinks likely to cause sickness).

Give the casualty the recommended dose of a simple painkiller such as paracetamol which will help to bring the temperature down.

Using medication – warnings

- Always follow the instructions on the packaging of the medication; if you have any doubts **seek advice** before giving the medication.
- Check if the casualty is taking any other form of medication, including those bought at a pharmacy or supermarket. If this is so, ***do not*** give anything else until you have sought advice. Seek advice from your doctor or local pharmacist.

Fever strip (left), mercury (centre) and digital (right) thermometers.

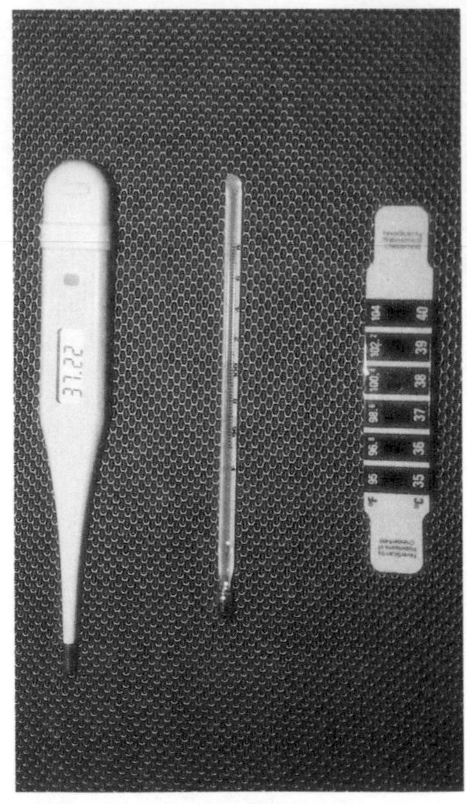

Fits

Fitting occurs when the normal electrical activity of the brain is disturbed, as in epilepsy, or when other parameters of normal brain functions are disturbed, as in a high fever.

A fit can be very upsetting to onlookers and, once over, very distressing to the casualty. Fits can occur anywhere and with little or no warning. They may last a few seconds or continue for some minutes. Whatever the cause and the duration of the fit, the basic first aid treatment is the same. (See also Fits in Children, p. 82.)

You may notice • Collapse.

- Rigidity and arching of the back.
- 'Foaming' at the mouth.
- Convulsions, either affecting the whole body or limited to a particular area.
- The convulsions may be in the form of violent jerking actions or restricted to twitching of the muscles.
- Apparent stoppage of breathing.

Treatment

Do not put or force anything into the casualty's mouth.

Do not try forcibly to restrain the casualty during the fit.

Remove any causes of danger from the casualty.

If possible, put soft padding into place around and under the casualty's head for protection.

Send a bystander to dial 999 for an ambulance.

Once the fit is over and the casualty's muscles have relaxed, check the ABC of Resuscitation (p. 6) and act accordingly.

If you can identify a possible cause to the fit you should alleviate this cause.

A person fitting in a disco: have the strobe and flashing lights turned off.

A young child or baby who has a high temperature: start to cool the casualty (p. 82).

REMEMBER

- The casualty, on waking up, will be aware that something has happened but may be disorientated and almost certainly distressed. If possible, disperse any onlookers so as to lessen some of the anxiety felt by the casualty.

Epilepsy

Epilepsy is a condition that causes fits and is subdivided into two main types: petit mal (minor) and grand mal (major). (In children, see p. 82.)

Petit mal

In this minor form of epilepsy brief disturbances of the brain's normal functioning cause a momentary loss of consciousness. Once the petit mal is finished, the casualty continues normal activity. Petit mal may precede grand mal fits.

You may notice • Apparent daydreaming.

• Staring ahead without awareness of surroundings.

• Twitching movement, particularly of the mouth, eyelids and head.

• Grinding of teeth, lip-smacking, chewing, rolling of the thumb on forefinger, etc.

TREATMENT

Remove any potential sources of danger from the casualty.

Offer reassurance until the casualty returns to normal.

Seeking medical advice

A casualty who is not aware of these sudden and brief episodes should be advised to see his/her own doctor.

Grand mal

This is the major form of epilepsy in which the casualty experiences fits with a period of unconsciousness. Many epileptics experience an 'aura' which warns them of an impending fit. For some, the 'aura' may be a petit mal, for others it can be by experiencing a particular smell or sensation.

In many cases, a grand mal fit has a number of phases that follow one after the other:

The casualty suddenly becomes unconscious and may cry out as this happens.

The casualty becomes rigid, often arching the back.

Breathing stops and, as the fit continues, the casualty becomes mostly cyanosed (blue) while the neck and face become red and congested.

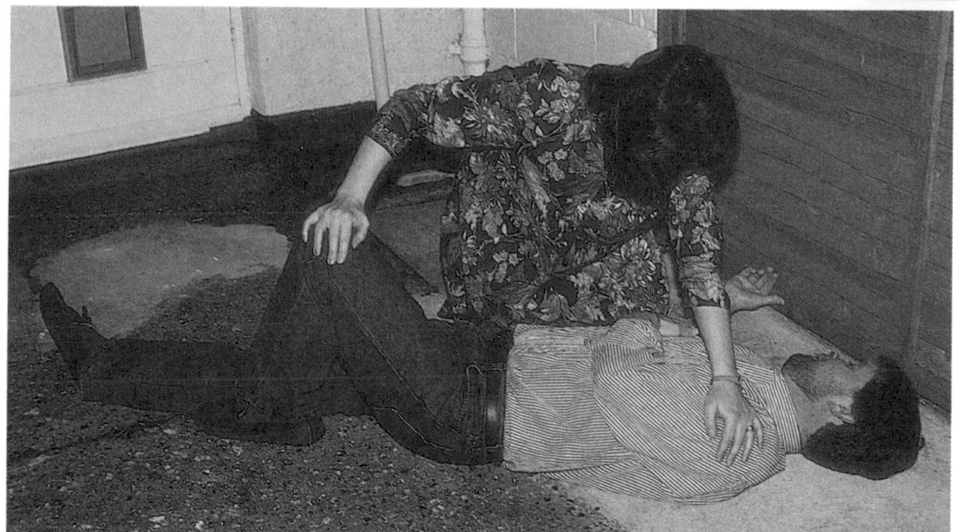

The convulsion proper begins with jerking and often violent movements of the limbs. The jaw is often clamped shut and the casualty 'froths' at the mouth; the saliva may be bloodstained if the tongue has been bitten.

The casualty may wet or soil him/herself.

The muscles relax and breathing returns. Initially, it may appear to be as occasional huge gasps but will quickly become normal.

The casualty rouses and may remain drowsy and disorientated for some time. Often, the casualty goes into a deep sleep before fully recovering.

Treatment

Do not use force to try to restrain the casualty.

Do not put anything in the casualty's mouth.

If possible, protect the casualty's head by placing something soft under it, e.g. clothing, cushion, etc.

When the fit ends and the casualty's muscles have relaxed, put him/her into the recovery position (p. 8).

When the casualty is able, take him/her somewhere in order to recover fully.

Dial 999: If the casualty does not regain consciousness after 5 minutes.

If the casualty is unknown to you and not accompanied by anyone.

If the casualty has a further fit.

If this is the casualty's first fit.

Status epilepticus

In this condition, the casualty does not recover and experiences a number of fits one after the other, not regaining consciousness between fits.

Treatment

Treat as for a grand mal fit.

Dial 999 for an ambulance.

Head Injuries

Head injury is a fairly broad term that covers any injury to the head and may involve impairment to the casualty's level of consciousness. All casualties suffering a head injury need to be seen by a doctor and often, if a period of unconsciousness has occurred, the casualty may be detained in hospital for observation. Scalp wounds, if present, will bleed profusely, and indicate the possibility of underlying damage. The single most useful indicator of a head injury is that the casualty suffers an altered state of consciousness.

Altered states of consciousness

There are four levels of consciousness usefully defined for the first aider, the most obvious being unconsciousness. A useful guide to determining a casualty's level of consciousness is to use 'AVPU'.

A – Alert	– Normal level of consciousness
V – responds to Voice	– Dazed/Semi-conscious
P – responds to Pain	
U – Unresponsive	– Unconscious

All unconscious casualties must be given an ABC of Resuscitation check (p. 6).

Compression

This occurs when pressure is exerted upon the brain. Because the brain is contained within the skull, any bleeding or swelling will cause a pressure build-up around the brain.

This is potentially a very serious condition that can become apparent immediately following a head injury or may be delayed for quite some time. As for other forms of head injury, medical attention is essential.

You will notice • A deterioration in the casualty's level of consciousness.

You may notice • A history of a recent head injury. It is possible that initially the casualty may have made an apparent full recovery.

- Disorientation/confusion.
- Intense headache.
- Unequal eye pupils.
- Breathing becomes slow and possibly noisy.
- Pulse becomes slow, but is strong and full.
- Hot flushed face.
- Raised temperature.
- Weakness on one side of the face or body.

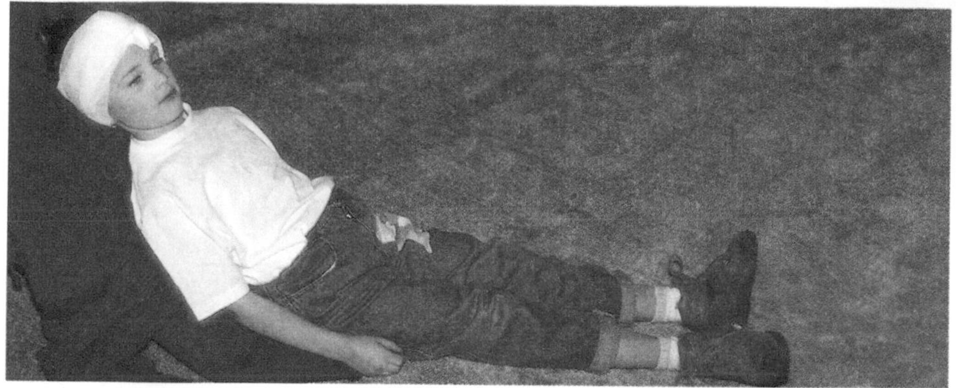

TREATMENT

If the casualty is unconscious, check the ABC of Resuscitation (p. 6).

If the casualty is fully or semi-conscious, provide support in a semi-sitting position.

Dial 999 for an ambulance.

Skull Fracture

The presence of a fracture of the skull is always indicative of a head injury. The bones of the skull surround the brain, providing protection. A skull fracture may be caused by direct force such as a blow to the head or by indirect force such as someone jumping down and landing heavily on the feet.

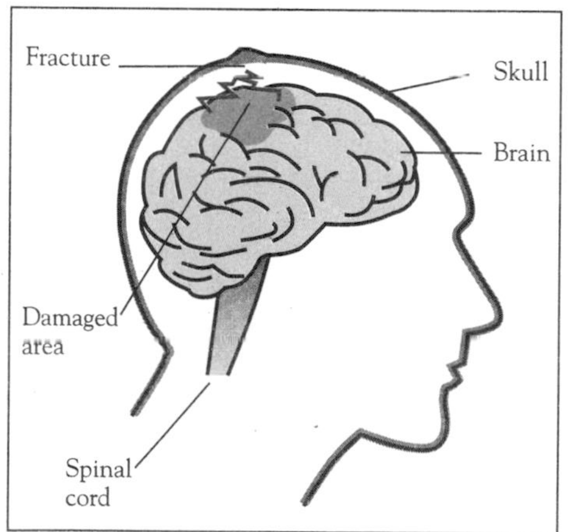

You may notice • Swelling.

- 'Boggy' area/depression on the head.
- Change in the shape of the head.
- A wound to the scalp.
- Blood in the white of the eye.
- Straw-coloured or bloodstained fluid from the nose or ear.

TREATMENT

If the casualty is unconscious, check the ABC of Resuscitation (p. 6) and act appropriately.

If the casualty is conscious, make him/her comfortable in a semi-sitting position.

If there is a discharge from the ear, apply a light pad and position the casualty so that the ear is able to drain (p. 98).

Dial 999.

Possible spinal injury

If you suspect a spinal injury, treat the casualty as described on p. 133.

Heart Problems

Heart disease is the single largest cause of death in the United Kingdom. The heart is a muscular pump that 'beats' regularly throughout life. Each heartbeat is the result of an electrical stimulation that originates from within the heart. Because it is a live organ the heart requires its own supply of blood that provides life-giving oxygen.

The most common cause of heart disease is ischaemia, a reduction in the amount of oxygen-carrying blood reaching the heart muscle due to a narrowing of the artery or arteries.

Angina

This is a cramp-like pain caused by a reduction in oxygen reaching the heart muscles. It may be brought on by exercise or excitement. For a relatively large number of people, angina is an ongoing problem that has a familiar pattern and responds to rest and medication.

You may notice • Crushing chest pain.

• The pain may spread into the jaw, arms and hands (particularly the left).

• A feeling of weakness.

• Tightening sensation in the jaw, arms and hand (particularly the left).

• A sensation of heaviness in the arms (particularly the left).

• Shortness of breath.

Treatment

Sit the casualty down on the spot.

Assist the casualty to take medication.

Allow the casualty to rest until completely recovered.

Dial 999: If the casualty does not normally suffer from angina.

If the pain is more intense or extensive than the casualty's normal angina pain.

If the pain does not respond in the normal way to rest and medication (i.e. persists or gets worse).

If the pain comes on when the casualty is at rest.

Heart Attack

A heart attack usually occurs because a part of the heart's muscle is suddenly starved of its blood supply, e.g. through a blood clot blocking an artery (coronary thrombosis).

You may notice • Central chest pain, often described as a tight band around the chest or intense pain under the breastbone.

• Abdominal discomfort, often initially thought to be indigestion.

• Breathlessness.

• Paleness, coldness and often excessive clamminess.

- Faintness or dizziness.
- Rapid, weak pulse (sometimes irregular).
- A feeling of impending doom.
- Sudden collapse into cardiac arrest.

Treatment

Always treat the casualty on the spot.

Make the casualty comfortable in a semi-sitting position, ensuring good support.

Dial 999 for an ambulance.

If available, call the casualty's own doctor; dial 999 for an ambulance **first.**

Stay with the casualty and be prepared to start resuscitation.

If you have an aspirin tablet readily available and the casualty is conscious and able to cooperate, give one tablet (it doesn't matter what the strength is) **to chew.** If the casualty has any objections to taking the aspirin (e.g. allergy) ***do not*** force the issue.

The Collapsed Casualty

- ☐ The first aider must be constantly aware of the casualty's overall condition particularly if he/she seems to settle and go to 'sleep'. Very often, collapse into cardiac arrest is sudden and unremarkable.

Heart Failure

This is a condition in which the heart muscle becomes inefficient and the circulation through the lungs becomes 'sluggish', causing fluid to gather there (pulmonary oedema). Heart failure may occur following a heart attack or be a symptom of other heart disease. The attacks often occur at night.

You will notice • Breathlessness, often severe.

You may notice • Paleness, coldness, clamminess.

Abdominal discomfort.

Central chest pain.

Blue tinge to the skin (cyanosis), especially the ears and lips.

Rapid deterioration, even to collapse.

Treatment

Help the casualty into a semi-sitting position and ensure good support.

Dial 999 for an ambulance.

If available, call the casualty's own doctor; dial 999 for an ambulance first.

Treating Chest Pain

- ☐ If the casualty is experiencing any chest pain during the 'attack', help him/her to take normal medication for relieving an angina attack.

Cardiac Arrest

This is the sudden and unexpected stopping of the heart's pumping action. It may be due to a heart attack or can be due to other conditions such as electrocution, heart failure or anaphylactic shock. Without the pumping of the heart, oxygen cannot be circulated and the heart muscle and the brain will rapidly be damaged. Carry out ABC of Resuscitation (p. 6).

Heat Problems

Body overheating from natural causes is a common occurrence in summer months and the effects should not be treated lightly.

Heat Exhaustion

This is a condition that develops gradually during prolonged and possibly unaccustomed exposure to heat, and results from heavy sweating, causing the body to lose salt and water (see also p. 84).

You may notice
- Malaise.
- Headache.
- Dizziness.
- Disorientation/confusion.
- Excessive sweating.
- Pale and clammy skin.
- Muscle and abdominal cramps.

TREATMENT

Take the casualty as soon as possible to a cool place.

Lay the casualty down and if possible raise and support the legs to improve blood flow.

Help the casualty to sip an isotonic drink or a very weak salt-water solution (one teaspoon in one litre of water).

Allow the casualty to rest until fully recovered.

If the casualty becomes unconscious or remains unwell despite the first aid procedures, dial 999 for an ambulance.

Heat Stroke

This is a potentially more serious condition than heat exhaustion. It often occurs suddenly and the casualty is in a state of shock or near complete collapse (see also p. 84).

You may notice
- Malaise.
- Nausea and vomiting.
- Disorientation/confusion.
- Hot, dry and flushed skin.
- A strong pulse.
- Rapid deterioration.
- High temperature of over 40°C (104°F).

TREATMENT

If the casualty is unconscious check the ABC of Resuscitation (p. 6) and act appropriately.

Remove the casualty to a cool place.

Take off all the casualty's clothing down to the underclothes.

Wrap the casualty in a cold wet sheet, keeping it moist.

Fan the casualty.

When the temperature has fallen to 37°C (98.4°F), dry the casualty and cover with a dry sheet; continue to fan.

Hypothermia

Hypothermia occurs when the body's temperature falls to 35°C (95°F) or below. It can be caused in a number of ways:

In the home: occurring over a number of days in homes that have little or no heating.

Out and about: prolonged exposure to the cold during outdoor pursuits is a common cause of hypothermia. If there is a cold wind, the 'wind chill' factor increases the risk.

Cold water: hypothermia due to immersion in cold water is rapid, up to 30 times faster than hypothermia occurring on dry land.

Special at-risk groups

Small children, particularly infants, are at greater risk from hypothermia because their ability to control their body temperature is poorly developed. Nor are they always able to say how they feel.

The elderly are at risk due to a number of factors that include lack of mobility, poorly heated homes, illness and poor diet.

The homeless are at considerable risk due to their circumstances, combined with illness and poor diet.

Resuscitation and Hypothermia

- Hypothermia can cause the lungs to become stiffer to inflate, so it may be necessary to perform resuscitation at a slower rate than normal.

You may notice • The casualty becomes apathetic, irrational and confused.

- Shivering.
- Cold, pale, dry skin.
- Lethargy.
- Slow, shallow breathing.
- Drowsiness.
- Gradual loss of consciousness.
- Slow, weak pulse.
- Collapse, even to the point of death.

Treatment (in the open)

Put further layers of clothing on the casualty.

Cover the casualty's head.

Remove the casualty to a place of shelter without delay.

Lay the casualty on a layer of dry, insulating material such as blankets, leaves, etc. OR

Put the casualty into a sleeping bag and provide warmth from your own body by lying alongside him/her within the bag (if necessary use newspaper, blankets or tent canvas instead of a sleeping bag).

Send for help – wherever possible, send two or more people to get help.

If the casualty is conscious, allow sips of warm drinks.

If the casualty becomes unconscious, turn into the recovery position (p. 8) and continue to provide warmth.

TREATMENT (in the home)

If the casualty is able to get into a bath **unaided,** immerse in a warm bath.

If the casualty is unable to get into a bath, remove any wet clothing.

Dress the casualty in a layer of warm clothing, including a hat.

Put the casualty into bed and provide extra covering.

Give the casualty hot drinks, preferably milky coffee or chocolate drinks.

DIAL 999

- If the casualty is unconscious.
- If the casualty is elderly or very young.
- If the casualty is disorientated or confused.

If the casualty becomes unconscious, place in the recovery position and continue to provide warmth until the arrival of the ambulance.

In all other cases where the casualty is not fully recovered after 1 hour, contact a local doctor.

Lifting and Moving Casualties

Lifting a casualty can be potentially very hazardous to the first aider. Also in those situations when an ambulance is required, movement of the casualty must be restricted to the minimum, i.e. into the recovery position.

There are situations, however, when it is necessary to move the casualty because of impending danger or to allow the first aider to perform vital life-saving techniques. The casualty with minor injuries may require assistance to move to a place of rest or a First Aid Centre.

When to move a casualty

If there is danger to the well-being of the casualty.

If life-saving skills cannot be performed where the casualty is found.

When minor casualties need to go to a place of rest or a First Aid Centre.

Principles of safe lifting

Any lifting should follow the principles given below:

1. Keep your back straight.

2. Bend at the knees.

3. Keep your feet comfortably apart, with one foot slightly in front of the other.

4. Keep the casualty (or object) you are lifting as close to yourself as possible.

5. Ensure a good grip, using the whole hand.

6. Never lift a casualty on your own if help is available.

7. Never assume a casualty can sit/stand without support.

8. Should you start to lose your grip or to overbalance, quickly but gently lower the casualty to the ground.

Cradle carry

Use this only with lightweight casualties.

Squat down by your casualty.

Put one of your arms around the casualty's waist, the other under the thighs.

Pull the casualty tight against you and lift.

Drag method

Use this method to evacuate a casualty rapidly from an area where there is danger. This lift may aggravate neck and head injuries and so should only be used to remove the casualty from extreme danger.

To remove the casualty by the drag method, cross the casualty's arms against the chest, if possible. As best you can, grasp the casualty's armpits and pull to safety.

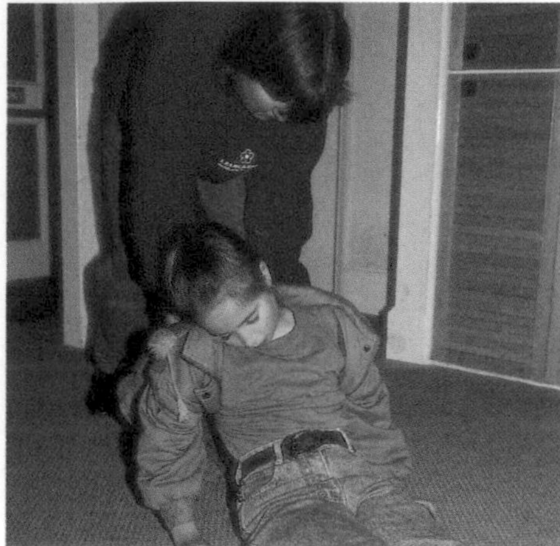

Alternatively, if the casualty is wearing a jacket or something similar, unbutton it and pull it under the casualty's head. Then grip the jacket under the shoulders and pull to safety .

If the casualty is able to sit up, ask him/her to cross their arms across the chest, put your arms under the casualty's armpits and firmly grip the forearms with your hands. Pull to safety.

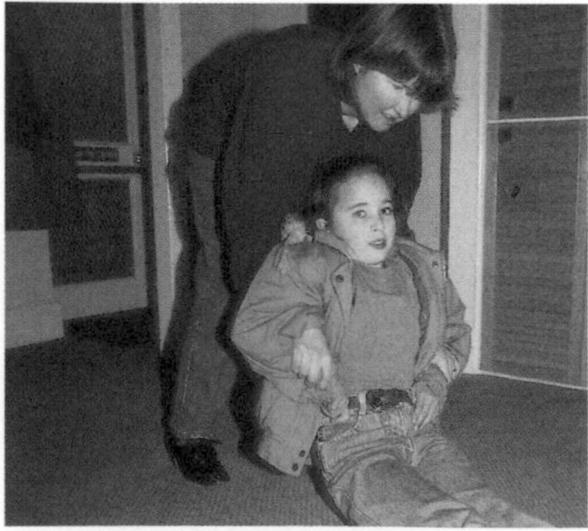

Pick-a-back

Use this lift for lightweight casualties who can, without any doubt, hold on to you.

Crouch in front, and facing away from, the casualty.

Ask the casualty to put his/her arms around your neck and to hold on by grasping both hands or your shoulders.

Get a good grip on to the casualty's thighs.

Rise slowly so as not to fall off balance; **keep your back straight.**

Human crutch

The casualty must be able to stand, to balance and to need minimal support whilst walking.

Stand on the casualty's uninjured side.

Ask the casualty to put his/her arm around your neck and grasp the hand (or waist) with your own hand.

Put your other arm around the casualty's waist and hold on to the casualty's waistband or belt.

Instruct the casualty to take small steps and not to hop or jump, which is likely to cause loss of balance.

GETTING A CASUALTY OUT OF A CAR

This should only be done for two reasons:

- There is life-threatening danger to the casualty if left in the car.
- If it is impossible to resuscitate the casualty in the car.

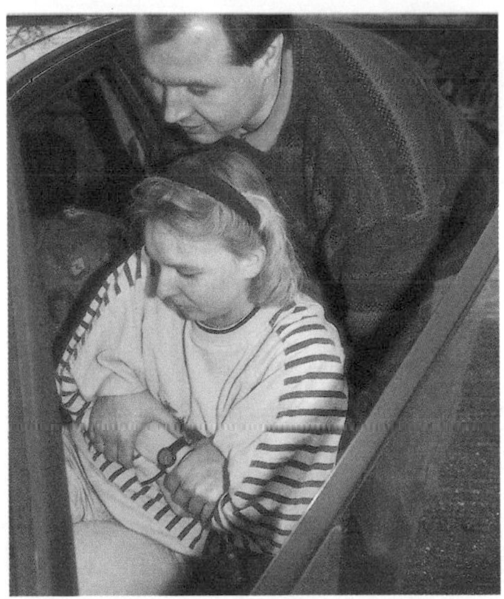

An unconscious casualty in a car should wherever possible remain inside the car for removal by the professional services. Attempt to keep the airway open by tilting the head back and lifting the chin forward (for children and infants the head tilt should be minimal).

If resuscitation is necessary, mouth to mouth can be performed with the casualty in the car. Chest compressions (if needed) are more of a problem and may require the casualty to be removed from the car.

As best you can, slide your hands under the casualty's armpits from back to front. Work from alongside the casualty.

If you can manage it, grasp the casualty's forearms with your hands; if not, get a good grip on the casualty's armpits.

In one movement lift casualty to the edge of seat.

Now drag casualty from the car to safety.

Miscarriage

A miscarriage is the loss of a foetus within the first 28 weeks of pregnancy. Statistically, approximately one-fifth of pregnancies will miscarry. In a number of cases the women concerned experience a late and heavy period without realising that they have been pregnant.

If a woman is aware she is pregnant and experiences a possible miscarriage, she is likely to be extremely concerned and upset.

If at all possible, a female first aider should tend to the woman; if this is not possible, the male first aider should try to obtain female support to act as a chaperone and to reassure the casualty.

You may notice • The woman complains of cramps in her lower abdomen, and within her pelvic area.

• 'Breakthrough' bleeding (i.e. spotting on pants).

• Heavy vaginal bleeding, often occurring very suddenly and accompanied by severe cramps.

• The woman passes large clots or other products of conception.

• Shock.

Treatment

Lay the woman down in a semi-sitting position with her knees propped up.

Provide a sanitary pad, small towel or something similar.

Ensure that any expelled material is kept out of the woman's sight. Keep it for inspection by the doctor or ambulance crew.

Reassure the woman and keep her warm.

Dial 999 for an ambulance.

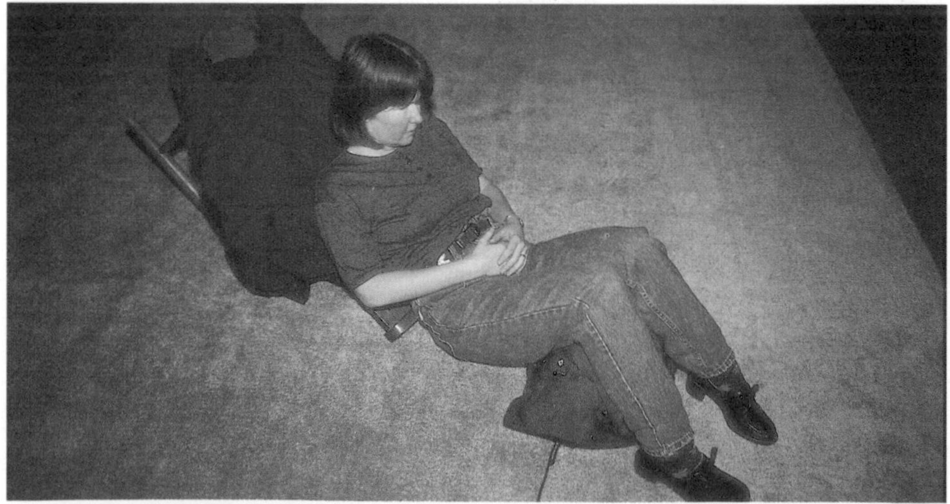

Nose Bleeds

There are a number of causes for a nose bleed. The most common is weakened nasal blood vessels during a cold. Others include a blow to the nose, heavy sneezing, blowing the nose, etc. People with high blood pressure may have a tendency to nose bleeds. (See also p. 52.)

Most usually, nose bleeds are minor events and, although irritating, are of no significance. Occasionally, bleeding can be very heavy and the casualty can lose a large amount of blood. In these cases maintaining an open airway becomes a priority, particularly if the casualty is unconscious.

If, following a head injury, there is a thin watery discharge that is bloodstained, **always** refer the casualty to hospital urgently.

Treatment

Sit the casualty down and tip the head forward so that the blood drains and does not run into the stomach, which may make the casualty sick.

Ask the casualty to pinch the fleshy part of the nose, just beneath the bony bridge.

Instruct the casualty **not to** sniff and to try not to cough or spit.

After 10-15 minutes let the casualty release the pressure on the nose. If it is still bleeding pinch the nose again for a further 10-15 minutes.

If available, an ice pad can be applied to the outside of the nose in addition to the pressure.

Once the bleeding has stopped, advise the casualty not to blow the nose for 4-6 hours so as to avoid dislodging the clot.

Do not attempt to 'pack' the nose with anything in attempts to stop the bleeding from within.

If the bleeding does not stop after 20-30 minutes, send the casualty to hospital. Throughout the journey the casualty should continue to lean forward and to pinch the nose.

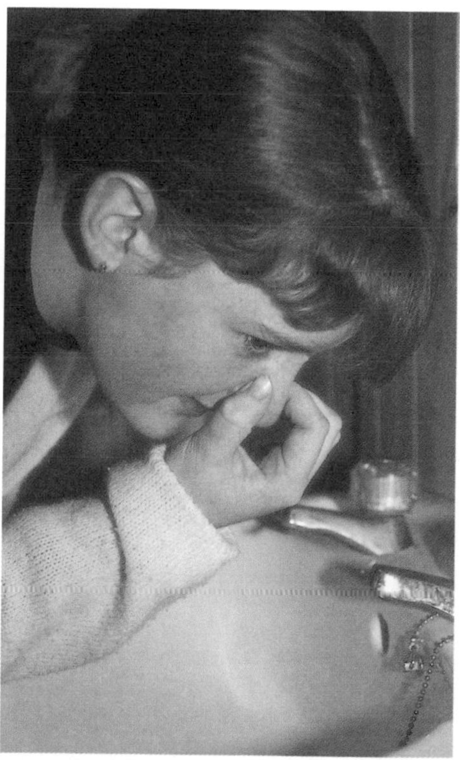

Overdose

Overdosing is a relatively frequent occurrence. Most people would assume that when someone takes an overdose it is a deliberate act intending to cause self-harm. Very often this is not the case. Accidental overdose occurs very easily, particularly amongst certain groups such as the elderly, children and those in a confused state brought on by alcohol or other drugs.

For some people, taking an overdose is a cry for help. They have little intention of causing any fatal self-harm but due to their state of very great emotional distress they resort to drastic measures. It is not uncommon for such people to seek to draw the attention of others to their actions.

Much less common are those who are intent on taking their own life. They often evolve elaborate plans which include a guaranteed period of seclusion and the taking of drugs that are highly likely to cause self-harm.

Whatever group your casualty falls into, your priorities are **always** the same. On occasions you may become aware of your casualty's actions because they inform you some time, even days, after taking the overdose.

It is a common misconception that if an overdose is to be fatal it will be so in a matter of hours. Whilst this is true for some drugs, it is not the rule and anyone who has overdosed should always be seen by a doctor.

Drug abusers deserve a special mention; they occasionally overdose due to the fact that their supply of drugs has been more highly refined than usual and is therefore of much stronger concentration, thus making an accidental overdose likely.

Treatment

If unconscious: Check the ABC of Resuscitation (p. 6). Act according to your findings.

If conscious: Dial 999 for an ambulance.

Stay with and reassure the casualty.

If the casualty becomes unconscious, treat as above.

Do not move the casualty around.

Do not try to make the casualty sick so as to empty the stomach of any remaining drugs. This can be very dangerous, even fatal.

Gather any evidence of what has been taken. This includes loose drugs, medicine bottles and any bottles of alcohol that may have been involved. Pass them on to the ambulance staff.

If help is refused

If the casualty refuses your help or does not want you to call for an ambulance, do not push the matter beyond simple reasoning. If necessary leave the casualty and dial 999 for an ambulance. The ambulance crew are in a better position to assess the casualty's needs and to negotiate accordingly.

Panic Attack

Some people respond abnormally when under stress or faced with an alarming situation, e.g. an accident or on hearing bad news affecting their family. The person becomes agitated and panicked and on occasion may be labelled by some as being hysterical.

You may notice • The casualty hyperventilates, with fast and unusually deep breathing.

• The casualty trembles; this can be so severe as to cause loss of coordinated movements.

• Sweating.

• Palpitations.

• Loss of control: shouting, screaming and displaying other unusual behaviour.

• Tingling in the hands.

• In extreme cases the casualty's hands may go into spasm.

Treatment

Remain calm at all times; you will need, however, to be firm in the initial stages, so as to gain their cooperation.

If possible remove the casualty from the stimulus to the attack; this will include any audience that has gathered, including concerned family and friends.

Encourage the casualty to control his/her breathing, by taking deep breaths at a slower rate and then gradually to take slower breaths until a near normal breathing pattern is achieved (see Hyperventilation p. 64).

Allow the casualty to talk about his/her anxiety, but not to become overwrought and unintelligible.

Encourage the casualty to become more composed before facing friends and family or returning to normal activities.

If the panic attacks are a frequent occurrence or related to some devastating personal tragedy, suggest that the casualty seeks medical advice.

Emotional responses

Some people, when faced with news affecting their family (good or bad), respond in a highly emotional way. This should not be confused with a panic attack.

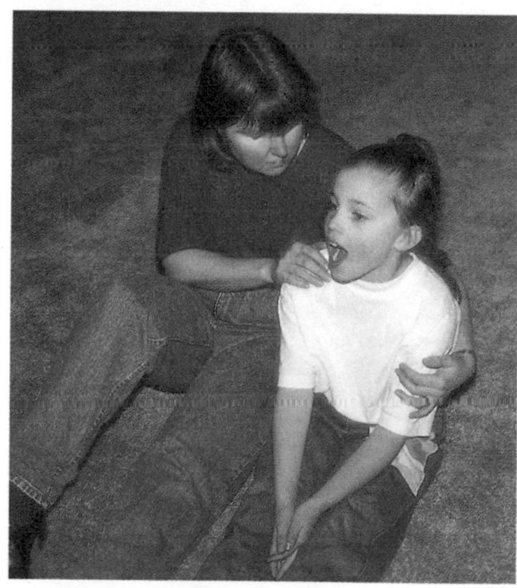

Penetrating Chest Wounds

Oxygen gets to the body through the lungs and for this to happen the lungs need to be able to expand. There is not normally any 'space' within the chest between the lungs and the ribs. During inhalation the chest wall moves out and the diaphragm moves down, stretching the lungs and drawing air down the windpipe.

If a wound to the chest – caused by stabbing, impalement, etc. – allows air to enter around the lungs (and not into the lungs as for breathing), there is a very great risk that this air will limit the lungs' abilities to expand. This is because if the air cannot get out of the chest space, it forms a physical barrier to normal lung expansion. If the lung cannot expand, breathing is hindered. (See also p. 58.)

You will notice • A wound in the chest.

You may notice • Breathlessness.

- Rapid shallow pulse.
- Difficulty in breathing.
- Blood bubbling out of the wound.
- Further blood being coughed up.
- The casualty becomes blue (cyanosis).

Treatment

Immediately cover the wound.

Help the casualty into a well supported semi-sitting position, **inclined** on to the injured side. (This allows the other lung to expand unhindered.)

Dress the wound by placing a small pad over the wound and then place an airtight seal over the top of that. Use a piece of plastic (even a plastic bag, cling film, etc.) and tape this down on **three** sides (leave the bottom untaped) so as to allow air to escape from the chest cavity but not to re-enter.

Dial 999 for an ambulance.

If the casualty is unconscious, place in the recovery position **injured side down**.

Improvised seals for a penetrating wound can include the following:

Plastic bag – either folded or cut to size.

Piece of plastic.

Credit card (or similar).

Note on sealing the wound

It is important to seal the wound on three sides, leaving one free. This will form a crude but effective one-way valve that is 'sucked' shut on inspiration so that air cannot enter the chest cavity and yet can be 'blown' open as air escapes during exhalation.

Poisoning

A poison is a substance which, if it gains entry into the body, can cause damage: this may be for a short period or may be permanent. Poisons can be taken into the body by a wide variety of routes.

Poisons can find their way into the body by being swallowed, inhaled, absorbed or injected.

The effects can vary greatly depending on the poison involved. Most commonly, poisoning occurs accidentally and involves ordinary substances that are found in and around the house. Poisoning can also be due to misuse of drugs, over-indulgence in alcohol or by eating food that is somehow contaminated.

Danger to the first aider

Particularly in cases of poisoning due to inhalation or absorption, the first aider must take every care not to become contaminated. On occasions it is necessary for the first aider to await professional rescue services rather than attempting a rescue independently.

Situations requiring special caution are those involving fumes, e.g. car exhaust fumes in a confined area, spillage of a chemical in a laboratory or when a container is leaking either fumes and/or fluid, e.g. from a tanker lorry involved in a road traffic accident. Remain upwind of the spillage and ensure that all bystanders do likewise.

Household poisons

Many common substances found in and around the home are poisonous. Hospital accident and emergency departments are only too familiar with young children being brought in after drinking disinfectant or other household chemicals. Certain substances, if spilt on to the skin (or splashed into the eye), can cause chemical burns to the skin.

Simple precautions around the home will greatly reduce the risk to children gaining access to household poisons:

- Fit the relevant cupboards with childproof catches.
- Store medicines out of the child's reach (remember they can drag chairs on which to climb).
- Do not store household solutions in old squash bottles; the child may help him/herself to a 'drink'.

Industrial poisons

Within the workplace many poisonous substances are in common use. Those industries that use potentially hazardous substances are required by legislation to provide notices that explain emergency action to be taken in case of an accident. In some cases, special first aid and medical facilities are required to be available; this will often include a specially trained rescue team.

Poisons that are swallowed

Do not try to make the casualty vomit.

If the casualty is unconscious check the ABC of Resuscitation (p. 6) and act accordingly.

If resuscitation is necessary, ensure that you are not contaminated by the poison – use a plastic face shield if available.

Dial 999 for an ambulance.

Remember to send the container with the casualty to hospital.

Inhaled poisons

If it is safe to do so, remove the casualty to fresh air.

If a specially trained rescue team is on site, **always** let them rescue the casualty. If this facility is not available and you consider the area unsafe to enter, await the arrival of the professional rescue service.

If the casualty is unconscious, check the ABC of Resuscitation (p. 6).

Dial 999 for an ambulance.

Poisons on the skin

If protective garments, e.g. gloves and/or smocks, are available always put them on before going to the casualty.

Flush away the chemical from the skin with copious amounts of water, using a hose or running water from a tap or shower.

Ensure that the chemical in the water does not further contaminate you or the casualty.

Dial 999 for an ambulance.

Special hazards in industry

Where special hazards occur, **always** ensure that you are fully conversant with the instructions for emergency action and that in the event of an accident you – **and others** – comply with the instructions under all circumstances.

Poisonous plants

Children are the most common victims of poisonous plants, being easily attracted to the bright berries.

If the casualty is unconscious check the ABC of Resuscitation (pp. 6, 15 and 19) and act appropriately.

Do not try to make the casualty vomit.

Dial 999 for an ambulance.

Try to identify the plant involved; ensure a sample is sent with the casualty to hospital.

Alcohol poisoning

Alcohol affects the central nervous system and thus the whole body in various ways. It is a depressant and causes a dulling of the senses, a deterioration in overall coordination and an altered level of consciousness.

Because of the effects of alcohol, the casualty who is severely impaired is at very great potential risk.

RISKS OF ALCOHOL POISONING

- An unconscious casualty may vomit and choke on his/her own vomit.
- Hypothermia has an earlier onset if the casualty collapses in a cold place.
- Other injury or illness may not be recognised, e.g. head injury, diabetes, epilepsy.

You may notice • A smell of alcohol.

- The casualty, if unconscious, may be easily roused but will quickly relapse into unconsciousness.
- Flushed face.
- Deep, often noisy, breathing.
- Full, bounding pulse.

In the later stages **you may notice**

- Shallow breathing.
- Wide, dilated pupils.
- Weak, rapid pulse.

TREATMENT

If the casualty is unconscious, check the ABC of Resuscitation (see p. 6) and act appropriately.

Even if conscious, place the casualty, for continuing safety, in the recovery position or at least on his/her side with a bolster down the back. This prevents the casualty rolling on the back and the risk of choking on his/her own vomit.

Ensure that the casualty is kept warm, placing a blanket (or similar) underneath as well as on top.

If you have any cause for concern regarding the casualty's condition, dial 999 for an ambulance.

Drug poisoning

Drug poisoning can occur as a result of an accident or following a deliberate overdose (p. 122). Any drug, no matter how common and easily available, is potentially a poison and must always be taken in accordance with the directions on the packaging. This will include the dosage, frequency of use and incompatibility with other substances – which almost invariably include alcohol.

COMMON DRUGS AND THEIR EFFECTS

Aspirin	Ringing in the ears, nausea and vomiting (may be bloodstained), upper abdominal pain, confusion.
Paracetamol	Effects become apparent some hours following ingestion; upper abdominal pain, nausea and vomiting, abdominal tenderness.
Tranquillisers	Lethargy and extreme drowsiness, unconsciousness, shallow breathing, abnormal pulse (may be fast or slow and may be irregular).
Hallucinogens and Stimulants	Extreme excitability, hyperactive behaviour, sweating, tremor of the hands, hallucinations.

TREATMENT

If the casualty is unconscious check the ABC of Resuscitation (p. 6).

Do not try to make the casualty vomit.

Dial 999 for an ambulance.

Send any empty containers (including alcohol) with the casualty to hospital.

Food poisoning

Poor food storage or handling may lead to food poisoning. Symptoms may be delayed for up to a day or so.

You may notice
- Nausea and vomiting.
- Abdominal cramps and diarrhoea.
- Weakness and even collapse.

TREATMENT

Encourage the casualty to lie down and provide a bowl in case of vomiting.

Seek medical advice.

Sexual Assault

Victims of a sexual assault may be either male or female, adult or child. Even the very young child is likely to be deeply shocked and psychologically disturbed. Sexual assault does not have to include penetrative sex, either vaginal or anal.
The victim may have other injuries apart from those around their genital areas and these may be potentially life-threatening.

No matter how minor the injuries or how 'minor' the assault, the sexual assault victim should always receive medical treatment. Unless the injuries are severe and require an emergency ambulance, medical examination should be arranged by the police.

Police evidence

As in other crimes, the police will need to gather all possible evidence. In the case of sexual assault much of the evidence will be found on and around the victim; the clothes may carry semen or bloodstains from the assailant, fibres and other material from the scene of the assault. The victim's body may well have evidence internally as well as externally (e.g. bruises).

It is extremely important that all evidence is preserved; do not put clothing into the washing machine or in to soak, etc. but if possible leave it on the person who has been assaulted. If the victim insists on his/her clothes being removed, place into a clean plastic bag (or similar). Advise the victim not to go to the toilet or to wash until he/she has been seen by the doctor. If you provide any covering such as a coat or a blanket, always ensure that the police are given this in a clean plastic bag if it does not accompany the victim to hospital or to the police station.

Sensitivity

The victim of sexual assault may very well feel threatened by you and others with you. He/she may well be in a terrible quandary and requiring help, yet will have an entirely understandable fear of others, particularly if of the same sex, build, etc. as the assailant.

Always be sensitive to the emotional needs of the victim and be aware that even the most innocent gesture or phrase can cause further distress.

Should the victim refuse all assistance, do not exert pressure.. Remember that he/she will be in a state of very severe emotional trauma. Try not to leave the victim alone, but as a priority ensure that someone summons the police and an ambulance.

Treatment

Treat any life-threatening injuries.

Reassure the casualty as much as possible.

Dial 999 for the police and an ambulance.

Preserve any potential evidence.

Advise the casualty not to go to the toilet or to wash.

Shock

Shock is a killer in its own right. It is often poorly understood and the term used inappropriately. In medical terms, shock occurs because there is a sudden lack of circulating oxygen available to the tissues. This can occur for a number of reasons, the most easily understood being shock due to blood or body fluid loss. The loss of blood or fluid can occur as a result of bleeding, burns, diarrhoea and vomiting. As the volume of circulating blood is reduced, the availability of oxygen transported to the tissues by the circulation is reduced.

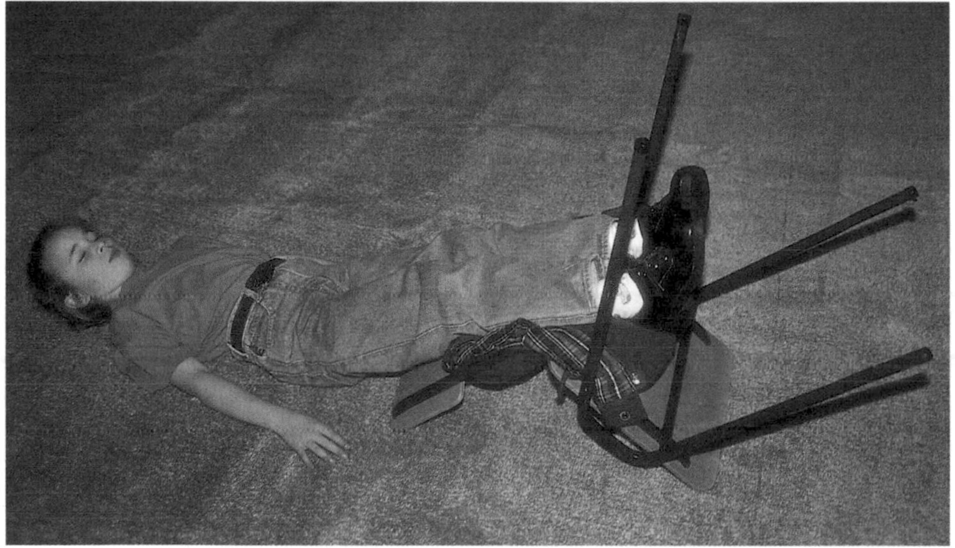

Following heart attack or heart disease, 'cardiogenic shock' is caused by the failure of the heart as an efficient pump to the circulatory system. This causes a 'sluggish' circulation of oxygen-carrying blood so that the supply to the tissues is not kept at the normal level.

In the case of an injury to the central nervous system, blood collects away from the vital centres of the body causing 'neurogenic' shock. There is a similar outcome when a casualty suffers a very large reaction as a result of allergy (anaphylactic shock).

In all situations where shock occurs, the essential organs are receiving lower levels than normal of oxygen. It is vital that treatment against shock starts as soon as possible. This will significantly improve the chances of survival for the severely injured/ill person.

Recognising the onset of shock is vitally important to the on-going well-being of your casualty.

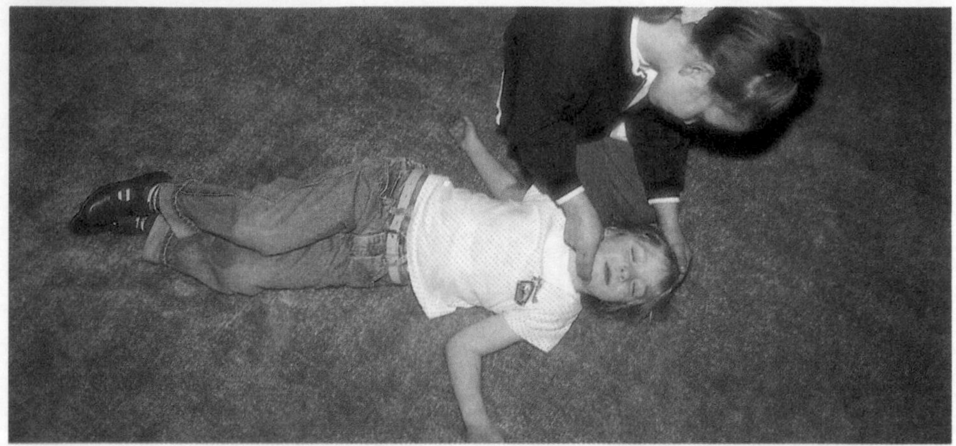

In the early stages you will notice

- Pale, cold and clammy skin.
- Fast pulse.

As shock develops you will notice

- Weakness.
- Lethargy and drowsiness.
- Thirst.
- Rapid, shallow breathing.
- Nausea and vomiting.
- Fast pulse (that may not be felt at the wrist as the shock becomes more serious).

As the brain becomes adversely affected you will notice

- Restlessness.
- Uncooperative manner, possibly aggression.
- Air hunger; yawning and gasping.
- Loss of consciousness.
- Respiratory arrest.
- Cardiac arrest.

Do not give the casualty anything to eat or drink.

Do not move the casualty unless life is endangered.

Treat the cause of the shock without delay, e.g. stop bleeding, etc.

Lay the casualty down.

Loosen tight clothing at the neck, chest and waist.

Raise the casualty's legs so that the feet are 1-2 ft (30-60 cm) above the ground.

Protect the casualty from the cold. Remember to place a blanket (or similar) underneath as well as on top.

Dial 999 for ambulance.

HEART ATTACK AND SHOCK

- If you suspect a heart attack (p. 112) it is most important that the casualty is **not** laid down but rather is supported in a semi-sitting position. The only exception to this rule is when the casualty becomes unconscious.

Skin Rashes

Skin rashes can occur for a number of reasons and may or may not require medical attention. In children rashes are often associated with the common childhood illnesses of measles or chickenpox (p. 87). Other causes may be allergy (p. 30) due to a food product, drugs, etc., or skin irritation following contact with a particular substance such as nettles, glass fibre or nylon, etc.

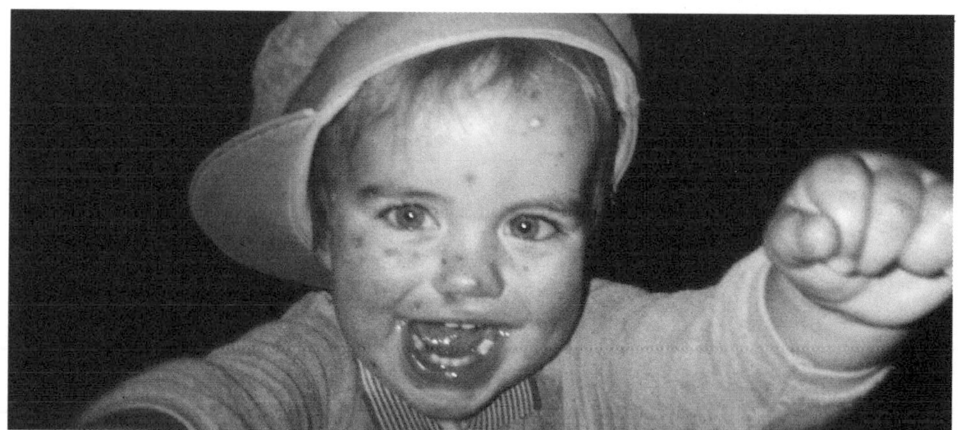

Certain medical conditions can involve rashes, the most common being eczema, psoriasis and shingles.

Skin rashes can vary from a small area of reddened skin to an extensive rash involving reddened skin, spots and open areas (usually associated with the casualty scratching to relieve itching). Often a rash is accompanied by irritation; sometimes the distress can be intense and cause loss of sleep.

If an open area develops, there is a risk that an infection may set in and cause further problems.

When to seek medical advice

When a rash is accompanied by other symptoms, e.g. fever, lethargy, pain.

If a rash may be associated with taking a drug or following immunisation.

If a rash is recurrent.

If the rash becomes infected.

If the rash causes distress or discomfort.

Treatment

Apply a cold compress over the full area of the rash.

Prevent the casualty from scratching; keep the finger nails very short and in the case of young children apply mittens.

Longer term relief for simple rashes may be obtained by applying liberal amounts of calamine lotion.

Spinal Injuries

Spinal injuries can be devastating in their long-term effects upon an individual. However, there are many myths and misconceptions surrounding the first aid treatment of casualties with a possible spinal injury.

YOU MUST ALWAYS

- Put the unconscious spinal injured casualty into the recovery position without delay (p. 8).

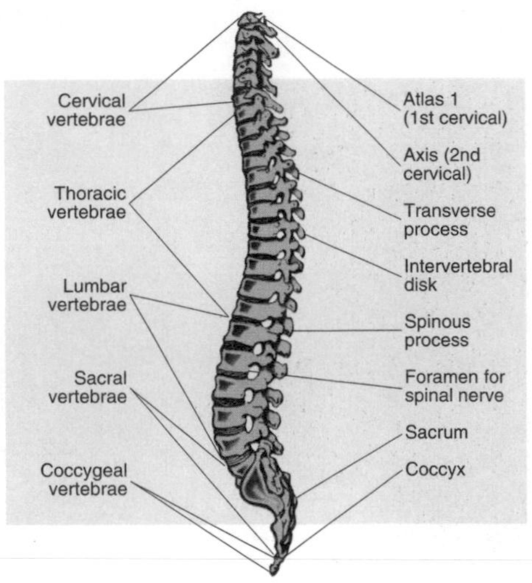

What is the spine?

In simple terms, the spine is a column of bones stacked on top of one another with a central canal running from the top to the bottom, through which the delicate spinal cord passes. The spinal cord is an extension of the brain and contains nerve fibres. Throughout the length of the spine nerves branch off and provide sensation and stimulus to move to different parts of the body.

The closer the spinal cord is to the brain, the more abundant are the nerve fibres within it. The spinal cord needs a constant supply of oxygen to function and this is provided by a network of blood vessels. The space through which the spinal cord passes in the bones is not very large and leaves no room for swelling to take place following injury.

The injured spinal cord

A normal response to any injury is swelling and the spinal cord is in this respect no different to any other part of the body. Unfortunately there just is not enough space in the passage through the bones to allow for this without causing other problems. As swelling occurs, the blood (and therefore oxygen) supply to the spinal cord becomes reduced; this will cause further swelling and worsening of any signs and symptoms.

Many victims of spinal injury may be spared serious effects if the first aider carries out three simple procedures at the scene of the accident, namely:

To ensure a clear airway.

To ensure optimum blood (and therefore oxygen) supply to the spinal cord.

To prevent further movement.

Recognising a spinal injury

It is important that with any accident you always consider the possibility of a spinal injury. There are certain types of accidents and injuries that should **always** alert the first aider to the possibility of a spinal injury:

A fall from a height.

A dive into shallow water.

A throw from a horse, motorbike or bicycle.

A head-on crash.

Any other road traffic accident that causes sudden or rapid deceleration.

A heavy object falling across the casualty's back.

Head/facial or chest injuries.

When treating a casualty who has suffered one of the above, always suspect a potential spinal injury – even if there are no other signs and symptoms.

You may notice

- Complaint of pain in the neck/back.
- An abnormal shape on examining the spine.
- Tenderness over part of the spine.
- Abnormal sensation of heaviness, stiffness, tingling, weakness.
- No sensation.
- Reduced, or loss of, control in the limbs.
- Difficult or abnormal breathing.
- Incontinence.

A clear airway for the casualty

Check inside the casualty's mouth for any obvious obstruction and remove.

Complete the ABC of Resuscitation checks (p. 6) and act appropriately.

If resuscitation is necessary move the head/neck with great care.

Optimum blood supply – the neutral position

This position should be used only for conscious casualties.

Gently move the casualty's head so that the nose and chin are in line with the breastbone and navel.

Move the head back **very gently** and **very slightly.**

Do not tilt the head back.

GOLDEN RULES

- ☐ **Never** pull or tug the casualty's head – turn with a slow smooth movement.
- ☐ ***Do not*** lift the casualty's head.
- ☐ ***Do not*** place your hand in the nape of the casualty's neck.

The unconscious casualty

GOLDEN RULES

- ☐ The unconscious spinal casualty **must** be placed in the recovery position.
- ☐ If the casualty's head is turned to one side, roll the casualty toward that side.
- ☐ Turn slowly and gently.

Check the ABC of Resuscitation (p. 6) and act as appropriate.

If you are alone, turn the casualty into the recovery position (p. 8).

If you have a helper, work together to turn the casualty into the recovery position. The two of you (**A** and **B**) should do the following:

A kneels at the top of the casualty's head and steadies it by putting the hands over the casualty's ears and holding the head still.

B kneels alongside the casualty on the side to which he/she is to be turned, straightens the casualty's legs, places the nearer arm out sideways with the elbow bent and the back of the hand lying on the ground.

B grips the casualty's thigh (just above the knee) on the opposite side and draws the leg up so that the foot rests flat on the ground alongside the other knee, continuing to support the leg that is propped up.

B brings the casualty's far arm across the body and supports it by holding it in place just above the elbow.

Working together, as **B** pulls the casualty over on to his/her side, **A,** who is supporting the head, controls it so as to ensure that the casualty's nose and chin are kept in line with the breastbone and navel and that the head **does not** fall to one side but constantly remains in the neutral position.

Do not pull on the neck.

Once the casualty is in the recovery position, it is very important that **A,** supporting the casualty's head and neck, **continues** to do so until the ambulance crew take over.

B stabilises the casualty by drawing the casualty's upper leg to a right angle at the hip and the knee.

B checks to see that the casualty is still breathing.

A small pillow can be slid into position under the casualty's head (without moving the head) so as to assist in maintaining the neutral position. This will help to keep the head and neck in a straight line and is **in addition** to the manual support which must continue as described on this page.

Rolled-up blankets (or similar) placed around the casualty's body will ensure greater stability.

The conscious casualty

GOLDEN RULES

- ***Do not*** move the conscious spinal casualty from the original resting position unless he/she is in danger or becomes unconscious.
- Tell the casualty not to move.

Kneel at the top of the casualty's head (if possible) and place your hands over the casualty's ears and hold the head steady.

Slowly and smoothly turn the casualty's head into the neutral position. ***Do not*** pull, tug or lift the casualty's head.

It is very important that the head and neck are manually supported in this position until the ambulance crew take over.

Send someone to dial 999 for an ambulance.

If possible, get another person to place padding around the casualty's body so as to prevent movement.

Sprains and Strains

Sprains and strains are 'soft tissue' injuries and affect the muscles and ligaments.
A sprain is an injury to a ligament, commonly caused by a wrenching movement at a joint that tears the tissues in the surrounding area.
A strain is a partial tearing of a muscle, often near a joint.

Very often it is quite difficult to be sure that a sprain or strain injury is not in fact a fracture. If you have any doubts at all as to whether there is a fracture, you must always assume the worst and treat it as such (p. 55).

Both sprains and strains can be extremely painful, severely affecting the ability to use the part involved, even to the point of not being able to bear weight should the injury be to the leg. Swelling can occur rapidly and be extensive and severe.

You may notice • Pain around the affected area.

- Stiffness of the affected area.
- Swelling and bruising.
- Difficulty in moving the affected part.

Treatment

Rest the injured part; sit or lay the casualty down.

Apply an ice pack around the injured part for 10 minutes, elevating the part while the ice pack is in place.

Apply a firm crepe bandage to the affected part (p. 40); remember to bandage from the joint below the injury to the joint above the injury. Always check to ensure that the circulation beyond the bandaged part remains normal.

If you have any doubt as to the severity of the injury, advise the casualty to seek medical advice.

Make an ice pack by:

Wrapping a bag of frozen vegetables in a towel (or similar).

Putting crushed ice into a plastic bag and sealing it; then wrapping the bag in a towel (or similar).

Stroke

A stroke affects the casualty's brain and is not always easy to recognise. Moreover, although most commonly associated with old age, it can occur earlier in life. It may be due to one of two causes.

One cause is a clot (thrombus) that blocks a blood vessel in the brain, causing an area to become starved of oxygen.

The other is due to high blood pressure or a weakness in the wall of a blood vessel in the brain, when a bleed occurs into the brain tissue. The bleed compresses the surrounding brain tissue.

In both cases the effects are worsened by the resultant swelling.

The brain is contained within the skull which is effectively a sealed box. This means that all the pressure caused by bleeding is directed into the delicate brain tissue, possibly with fatal effects.

The brain is the computer centre of the body and each part is dedicated to a particular function. Some of these functions are essential to life and any disruption within these areas can lead to death. In other cases the casualty (if conscious) may have paralysis of one or more limbs, disrupted vision or speech, or any number of other symptoms. It may be that the casualty is able to move normally but appears confused (p. 90).

You may notice • Sudden and severe headache.

- Confusion.
- Drowsiness.
- Unconsciousness.
- Weakness or a paralysis (often confined to one side of the body). This includes dribbling, lop-sided mouth, slurred speech, loss of power or movement in the limbs, incontinence.
- Loss of speech.
- Loss of coordination.
- Vagueness or loss of concentration.

Treatment

If the casualty is unconscious check the ABC of Resuscitation (p. 6) and act appropriately.

If the casualty is conscious lie him/her down with head and shoulders raised to 3-4 pillows' height.

Dial 999 for an ambulance.

Transient Attacks

☐ Sometimes people suffer a stroke that can include paralysis, loss of consciousness or less severe symptoms, but make a full recovery within a short space of time. Casualties who suffer these short 'transient' strokes should always be seen by a doctor, preferably as a matter of urgency. Keep them at rest, even if apparently fully recovered, until seen by the doctor.

Sunburn

Sunburn is literally a burn caused by the sun (see aso p. 84). Over-exposure can cause severe burns and considerable discomfort. Sunburn can also be caused by sunlamps and sunbeds. Certain prescribed drugs can make the skin more sensitive to the sun and cause earlier and more rapid sunburn.

For sunburn to occur, it is not always necessary for it to be a bright and sunny day. "Skyshine" can cause serious burning. Many skiers have become sunburned due to the reflection of the sun off the snow.

You will notice • An area of red skin associated with slight discomfort (mild sunburn).

• An area of intensely red skin associated with more severe discomfort and pain that radiates heat (severe sunburn).

You may notice • Blisters.

• Heat stroke (p. 114).

Treatment

Do not apply oils and poultices made from fatty substances, e.g. butter, margarine, etc. These will only serve further to intensify the burning just as surely as if they were being used in a frying pan.

Remove the casualty from the sun into a place of cool shelter so as to obtain immediate relief from the heat.

Cool the area by applying cold water; for larger areas, soak non-fluffy materials in cold water and lay them over the affected area. Continue cooling until relief is achieved.

If blisters are present ***do not*** attempt to burst them (this can cause a serious infection). Cover them with a light dressing.

If blisters are present or the casualty remains in severe discomfort, seek medical advice. If you suspect heat stroke, dial 999 for an ambulance.

Minor sunburn

- ☐ Advise or assist the casualty to use a proprietary after-sun lotion or calamine lotion on the affected area.

A word of warning Babies, young children and the fair-skinned are most at risk from the effects of the sun (p. 84). Whereas to many people a 'healthy tan' may be the symbol of a good holiday, it is well proven that skin cancer tends to occur in those who regularly expose themselves to the sun.

Teeth

Far from being inanimate lumps of solid white material that are arranged across our upper and lower jaws, teeth are living matter. Problems affecting the teeth can have considerable consequences beyond the obvious pain and discomfort.

Wherever possible dental problems should be dealt with by your dentist, but where this is not possible, telephone your nearest Accident and Emergency Department to ascertain if there is any emergency dentist that you can contact.

Toothache

Toothache can be very uncomfortable and on occasions even debilitating.

Dental decay usually results in a steady pain that may be made worse by a hot or cold drink or food, whereas a dental abscess (infection) is distinguished by intense throbbing pain sometimes combined with bad breath.

Treatment

Advise the casualty to hold a covered hot water bottle in place over the affected side of the jaw.

If necessary, give the recommended dose of a simple painkiller such as paracetamol (for children use paracetamol syrup.) Do this only if the casualty has not taken anything similar within the last 4 hours and has not been drinking alcohol.

Arrange for an early dentist's appointment.

Lost filling

Toothache can be the result of a filling having fallen out.

Treatment

Plug the cavity with a piece of cotton-wool that has been soaked in oil of cloves.

Give simple painkillers as described, and make a dental appointment.

Tooth knocked out

With prompt and efficient first aid and urgent dental treatment, knocked-out "adult" teeth can be successfully reimplanted in both children and adults.

Treatment

If possible immediately replace the tooth in the socket, and advise the casualty to keep the teeth tightly together so as to splint it in place.

Alternatively, place a rolled gauze pad over the socket if it is bleeding heavily.

The tooth should be placed inside the casualty's cheek or in a glass of milk.

Send or take the casualty (with the tooth) to a dentist or hospital immediately.

Varicose Veins

The veins of the legs contain a series of one-way valves which ensure that the blood continues to flow toward the heart rather than backflowing. In some people, one or more of the valves become leaky. As a result, part of the vein becomes distended and appears as a blue knobbly vein just under the skin. The walls of the vein are overstretched and consequently are fragile. Light knocks can rupture the vein and profuse bleeding occurs.

Treatment

Lay the casualty down and raise the leg as high as can be tolerated.

Apply direct pressure on to the bleeding point.

Apply a sterile dressing (p. 42). Keep the leg raised.

Loosen or remove any constrictive clothing from the affected leg.

Dial 999 for an ambulance.

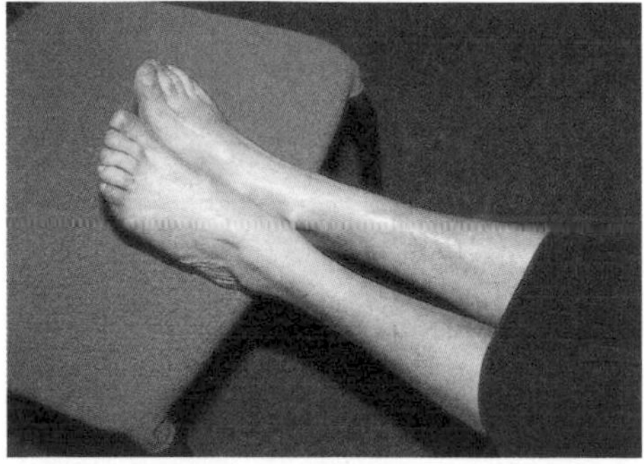

Kneel down by your casualty and place the foot of the injured leg on your shoulder; this elevates the leg extremely well and allows you to apply direct pressure.

Appendix

Learning first aid

This book is a guide to first aid and whilst it covers the various injuries and illnesses that may occur, it does not give you practical experience and tuition. This can only be obtained by attending a first aid course.

Training organisations

British Red Cross (all of UK).

St John Ambulance (not Scotland).

St Andrew's Ambulance Association (Scotland only).

Order of Malta (N. Ireland)

Short courses

Some organisations run short courses that cover the essential life-saving skills.

British Red Cross.

St John Ambulance.

St Andrew's Ambulance Association.

Local Heartstart/Heartguard Organisations.

Some Ambulance Services/Trusts.

Numbers for the above organisations can be found in local telephone directories.

Your own first aid kit

It is useful and sensible to keep a well-stocked first aid kit in your house and the car. Kits can be bought complete or compiled by yourself.

ITEMS	HOME	CAR
Triangular bandage	2	4
Small sterile dressings	2	
Medium sterile dressings	2	2
Large sterile dressings	1	2
Extra large sterile dressings		2
5 or 7.5 cm crepe bandage	1	
10 cm crepe bandage	1	
Assorted plasters	12	12
Antiseptic wound wipes	6	6
Eye pads	2	2
Safety pins	6	6
Torch	1	1
High visibility/reflective jacket		1
Seatbelt cutter/windscreen hammer		1

Getting help

When someone is ill or injured it is important to obtain help. However, it is not always necessary to dial 999; other agencies may be able to help.

Pharmacist

The local chemist's shop will invariably have a pharmacist on duty during shop hours who will be able to offer advice on suitable non-prescription remedies. The pharmacist will also inform you if certain medications cannot be taken together.

Midwife

If a woman is experiencing problems associated with her pregnancy, it is well worth contacting the midwife; often there is a central number to ring so as to speak to a duty midwife. She will be able to offer advice and if necessary arrange for a doctor to call and check the pregnant woman's condition.

Health visitor

Your health visitor can offer advice on health care matters relating to babies, children and the elderly. She can usually be contacted by leaving a message at your local family doctor's reception.

Nurse

A nurse will be found at your local health centre and increasingly at many doctors' surgeries. She can be contacted by phone for advice and in some areas a 'drop in' minor casualties clinic is available.

Family doctor

Your GP (or deputy) is available 24 hours a day, 7 days a week and can be contacted by phone for advice. During surgery hours ask the receptionist for guidance on the best time to phone. At other times ring the 'on-call' number. For non-urgent health problems where it is appropriate to see the doctor, you should book an appointment. If necessary, such as when you suspect an infectious disease or the casualty is debilitated, request that the doctor makes a home visit.

First aid posts

Many public venues and large workplaces have first aid facilities available. These may be manned by members of voluntary organisations such as the British Red Cross or an employee may be 'on call'.

Accident and Emergency department

A self-referral system is operated so that anyone can seek emergency treatment at the local A and E department. However, remember that the department is set up to deal with accidents and emergencies, not routine health matters. It is not an alternative to registering with or waiting for an appointment with your family doctor.

Emergency Ambulance Service

This service is obtained by dialling 999. It should only be used for casualties who, due to a serious illness or injury, need hospital treatment. For minor injuries, such as cuts that need stitching and possible fractures to the arm, every reasonable effort should be made by the casualty to arrange his/her own transport. However, it must be stressed that if you are in any doubt at all as to whether an ambulance is required, dial 999 without delay.

Index

This book was created by Amazon Publishing Ltd

Editor: John Gilbert Design: Glynn Pickerill Illustrations: C.R. Oakes
Typesetting and Production: The R & B Partnership

Published by Blitz Editions, an imprint of Bookmart Ltd, Registered Number 2372865
Trading as Bookmart Ltd. Desford Road, Enderby, Lèicester LE9 5AD
ISBN 1 85605 196 X Printed in the Slovak Republic
50987